Choosing Your GCSEs

Choosing Your GCSEs

Alan Vincent
11th Edition

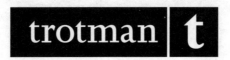

Choosing Your GCSEs

This 11th edition published in 2010 by Trotman, an imprint of Crimson Publishing, Westminster House, Kew Road, Richmond Surrey TW9 2ND

Author: Alan Vincent

10th edn published as *Choosing Your GCSEs & Other Post-14 Options* in 2007 by Trotman Publishing
9th–5th edns published by Trotman & Co Ltd in 2004, 2002, 2001, 1998 and 1995 as *How to Choose Your GCSEs: Essential Information about Key Stage 4 Courses and Examinations*
4th edn published by Trotman & Co Ltd in 1993 as *Your GCSE Decisions*
3rd edn published by Trotman & Co Ltd in 1990 as *Your GCSE Decisions* by G Thomas and Alan Vincent
2nd edn published by Trotman & Co Ltd in 1989 as *Your GCSE Decisions* by G Thomas, Clive Carpenter and Alan Vincent
1st edn published by Careers Consultants in 1987 as *Your GCSE Decisions* by G Thomas

British Library Cataloguing in Publication Data
A catalogue record of this book is available from the British Library

ISBN: 978-1-84455-212-2

Typeset by RefineCatch Limited, Bungay, Suffolk

Printed and bound in the UK by TJ International Ltd, Padstow, Cornwall

Contents

PART THREE: END NOTE

About the author

Alan Vincent is General Secretary of the Association for Careers Education and Guidance (ACEG). Initially a languages teacher, he has also worked as Head of Careers in a secondary school, Head of Guidance and Admissions in a 16–19 consortium, as an Education Business Partnership Manager and as a 14–19 Consortium Coordinator. He has extensive experience in educational and vocational guidance for young people and was a secondary school governor for more than 20 years.

Alan is the author of several books, including *Look Ahead: a Guide to Working in Sport* and *Look Ahead: a Guide to Working Abroad* and articles in a wide range of careers publications.

Introduction

By the time you read this book, you have probably spent something like 7 years in school. You may have changed schools once or twice already – and these seemed quite big hurdles to overcome at the time. But now the decisions that lie ahead will be even more important for your whole future. Also, because you are older and know more about yourself and the sort of person you are and want to be, you will have more say in making these new decisions.

The decisions you make now will affect your pathway through life. They will influence the choices you make at age 16 and later – the choices of A levels, of further education or training courses, and of an eventual job or career.

This book gives you details of the most popular GCSEs and other courses that are likely to be available, so that you can make an informed choice. Here are some of the questions that you may have and this book can help answer.

- What GCSEs are available?
- What are the other Key Stage 4 options?
- How can I choose between the different courses?
- Which GCSEs do I need to study for my possible post-16 choices?
- What do I learn in particular subjects?
- How do subject choices affect my career?

Getting the right answers to these questions is very important: poor or hurried decisions at this stage can have consequences later on. With the help of this book, you should be able to find your way through the maze of qualifications that are available and make the choices that are best for you.

The main focus in this book is on GCSEs and other courses common to England, Wales and Northern Ireland.

How to use this book

Part One of the book is about the different post-14 or Key Stage 4 options available. Part Two gives details of GCSE subjects, and any other courses available at this stage. The final part looks at how to make your studies a success and includes information on how exam boards assess GCSE and other courses. Part Three – the end note – explores some of the options that will be open to you at age 16.

If you're not sure of the meaning of any of the terms used in the book, you can refer to the glossary of terms and abbreviations on page xiii. The first mention of each glossary term or abbreviation in the text is highlighted in bold.

Just as everybody learns in a different way, people read books differently. Some like to read them from cover to cover; others prefer to start with the section that seems most relevant to them. You can approach this book in either way. If you need a complete introduction to Key Stage 4 courses, it would be a good idea to read through the book and make a note of the important points. If you already have some knowledge but need help with a particular issue, then the following table should help point you to the most relevant areas:

Table 1

	GCSE (or equivalent) issue	Which section of the book?
1	I'm not sure whether I ought to concentrate entirely on GCSEs or whether to take at least one applied or vocational course	See *What are the options?* and *Choosing your qualification* in Part One, pages 3 and 19
2	I need to find out about the different kinds of Key Stage 4 qualification	See *What are the options?* and *Choosing your qualification* in Part One, pages 3 and 19
3	I can't decide which subjects to take and which to give up. How can I choose?	See *Choosing your subjects* in Part One, page 19
4	I know I want to carry on later and take A levels but I'm not sure which GCSEs to take	See *Choosing your subjects* in Part One, page 23; and Part Two
5	I want to find out details about each GCSE subject	See Part Two
6	I want to spend part of my time in a college of further education	See *Choosing your qualification* in Part One, page 3; Part two, page 35; and *End note: What next?* in Part Three, page 147

Glossary of terms and abbreviations

Term/abbreviation	Definition
A level	Advanced level
A2	Advanced level – the second half of a full A level
Additional and specialist learning	This includes optional subjects that students can choose when doing a Diploma. The idea is to give students the opportunity to broaden their studies. This learning element includes qualifications in specific occupational areas (specialist learning) or other areas of study (additional learning), depending on the individual student's abilities and aspirations
AEA	Advanced Extension Award
Apprenticeship	A way for young people to train while working in particular skilled areas
AS	Advanced Subsidiary level. Forms the first half of a full A level, but is also a qualification in its own right
Application of number	This skill helps you improve your number skills
ASDAN	Award Scheme Development and Accreditation Network
BTEC	Business and Technology Education Council (part of Edexcel Foundation)
CACHE	Council for Awards in Children's Care and Education
Careers Wales	An all-Wales service that gives people of all ages free careers information, advice and guidance
CCEA	Council for the Curriculum, Examinations and Assessment (Northern Ireland)
CoPE	Certificate of Personal Effectiveness
Critical skills	Analysing or commenting on other people's work. Note that 'critical' in this sense does not mean criticising but looking for both good and bad points
Curriculum development organisation	An organisation involved in developing a syllabus of study for a course
CV	Curriculum vitae (a summary of your achievements and other details of your life relating to an application for a course or employment)
DCSF	Department for Children, Schools and Families
Diploma	A new qualification to recognise achievement at ages 14–19, combining practical skill development with theoretical and technical understanding and knowledge
DipSW	Diploma in Social Work
Edexcel	One of the main exam boards in England

Enterprise skills	See 'Entrepreneurial skills'
Entrepreneurial skills	The skills required to set up your own business, e.g. willingness to take a risk or start a new project
Ethics/ethical issues/values	To do with what is believed to be good and what is considered to bad, specially in relation to work, e.g. running a business, being a doctor or a lawyer
Evaluative skills	These skills help you to assess information, to give your opinion on the value of other people's work and ideas and to have confidence in your own decisions
Fast Tomato	Careers and course information software program
FE	Further education
Framework	What a course is based on
GCE	General Certificate of Education
GCSE	General Certificate of Secondary Education
Generic learning	This includes the areas of learning that are common to all lines of learning when doing a Diploma, e.g. English, Maths, ICT
IB	International Baccalaureate
ICT	Information and Communication Technology
Investigative work	A particular type of practical work in the sciences that is based on the principle that answers to all questions need proof
Kudos Online	Careers information and matching software program (from CASCAiD)
Learning line	Subject of study
NHS	National Health Service
NVQ	National Vocational Qualification
NQF	National Qualifications Framework
Occupational area	A range of occupations that share something in common, e.g. health care is an occupational area
OCR	Oxford, Cambridge and Royal Society of Arts Examining Board
Partnerships (or consortia)	Groups of schools and colleges that work together to increase the range of their curriculum offering
Portfolio	A folder containing the evidence that shows you have developed the necessary skills for a particular piece of work
Principal learning	This includes the knowledge, understanding and skills that are specific to a particular subject and are compulsory to learn. It also includes developing an awareness of any current issues related to the subject. Half of the principal learning content must be delivered through work-related learning
QCDA	Qualifications and Curriculum Development Agency
Scheme of work	A teacher's way of breaking up the work to be done in a whole year into manageable chunks or units of work

Specification	An outline of the course of study produced by exam boards
State-maintained schools	Schools funded by the government
Syllabus	See 'Specification'
Technical certificates	Certificates that are awarded to people who complete a specialised course of study that is related to specific vocational skills.
Training providers	These organisations organise work-based training with employers. Some specialise in certain types of training (e.g. business administration or IT), whereas others cover a broader range of occupational areas. Some also provide their own in-house training
UCAS	Universities and Colleges Admissions Service
Vocational	To do with a career or a job
Work-based training	Training in a particular occupational area with an employer in the workplace
Work-related learning	Learning within and outside the curriculum about the world of work

PART ONE

OPTIONS AND DECISIONS

CHAPTER ONE

What are the options?

This chapter covers an outline of the main Key Stage 4 courses and qualifications.

In this chapter we will be looking at all the options available to you at Key Stage 4 level. These are:

- **GCSEs**
- Applied GCSEs
- Short course GSCEs
- **Diplomas**
- Entry level qualifications
- **BTECs**
- **OCR** Nationals
- City & Guilds qualifications
- Young **Apprenticeships**
- **ASDAN**
- **NVQ**s
- Key Skills
- Functional Skills.

Note: These are all the options available, but you will need to check which ones out of these are offered in your school.

Jargon Buster: Key Stage 4

Key Stage 4 is the term used to describe Years 10 and 11 in secondary schools. Normally, this is when you prepare for examinations taken towards the end of Year 11. However, preparation for some exam courses now starts in Year 9, possibly even earlier, and many younger students are following Key Stage 4 courses in one or more subjects. So we have chosen to refer to Key Stage 4 rather than ages 14–16 in this book.

Compulsory subjects

During Key Stage 4 there are some subjects that everyone has to take, but others are optional – you can choose whether to take them or not. All students have to take:

- English
- Mathematics
- Science
- **ICT**.

These subjects are part of the National Curriculum and they will help you build up the skills you will need in the future, such as reading and writing clearly, being able to use numbers, and problem solving. For most students, it means taking the subject as a GCSE, but your teachers will advise you if an entry qualification instead in one or more of these subjects might be more suitable for you.

If you go to school in Wales, you will also have to study Welsh. In addition, everyone has to study careers education, citizenship, physical education (PE), religious studies, sex education, and **work-related learning**. However, you may not have to take exams in these subjects. Some schools also have other compulsory subjects. Check whether your school has other compulsory subjects and what they are.

Jargon Buster: National Curriculum

The National Curriculum is a **framework** used by **state-maintained schools** to ensure that teaching and learning is balanced and consistent for all learners aged 5–16. These schools have to provide a balanced and broad-ranging curriculum that:

- promotes the spiritual, moral, cultural, mental and physical development of their students
- prepares their students for the opportunities, responsibilities and experiences of adult life.

The National Curriculum sets out:

- the stages and core subjects to be taught at each stage – the knowledge, skills and understanding required in each subject
- the standards or attainment targets for each subject.

Science

There are three ways to take GCSE Science.

- You can take all three sciences separately – Biology, Chemistry and Physics.
- You can take 'Double Science', which combines parts of those three subjects.

- You can take 'Single Science' but bear in mind that this option is intended *only* for a minority of pupils who have good reason to spend more time on other subjects.

You can read more about these three ways of taking GCSE science on page 96.

GCSEs

The GCSE is the main way of assessing your attainment at the end of compulsory secondary education. GCSEs are available in more than 45 subjects, including eight 'applied' (work-related) subjects. The GCSE examination is available to all students at 16+ (and in some cases, earlier).

GCSEs mainly involve theoretical study, but there is also some **investigative work**. For example, in GCSE Leisure and Tourism you might be asked to find out about local providers, what services and facilities they offer, how much they charge, how their customers rate them, etc. Some subjects will also involve some practical work.

All GCSEs have to provide opportunities for you to develop – and be assessed on – the main Key Skills (communication, **application of number** and information technology). There are different levels of Key Skills, and your school will decide which level is correct for you. Depending on the subjects you take, you will also have opportunities for developing and being assessed in the 'wider' Key Skills: working with others, improving your own learning and performance, and problem solving.

Some facts about GCSEs

- There are more half a million entries for GCSEs in England, Wales and Northern Ireland each year.
- Results continue to improve and in 2009 more than two in three grades were between an A* and a C.
- More than one in five exams taken resulted in the award of an A* or A grade. The overall pass rate (A*–G grades) was 98.6%.
- More girls get A*s and As than boys.

GCSEs also have to help you in other aspects of learning that are considered essential to the National Curriculum, including:

- environmental issues
- **ethical values**
- European issues
- health and safety
- spiritual, moral, social and cultural development.

GCSEs are usually assessed by a mixture of examinations and other forms of assessment, with grades awarded in the range A*–G (with A* being the highest grade).

As part of the recent changes to the GCSE in England, instead of doing unsupervised coursework, you now will have to do what is called 'controlled assessment'.

What is controlled assessment?

Controlled assessment keeps the advantages of coursework while ensuring that work that you submit is your own. The key feature of controlled assessment is still the same as coursework – that students should be actively involved in learning. The following list gives the percentage of marks that controlled assessment contributes to the total in the revised **specifications**.

Subjects without controlled assessment:

- Classical Greek
- Economics
- Latin
- Law
- Maths
- Psychology
- Religious Studies
- Sociology.

Subjects with 25% controlled assessment:

- Business Studies
- Classical Civilisation
- Geography
- History
- Humanities
- Statistics.

Subjects with 60% controlled assessment:

- Applied Business
- Art and Design
- Citizenship Studies
- Construction and the Built Environment
- Dance
- Design and Technology
- Drama
- Engineering
- Expressive Arts
- Health and Social Care
- Home Economics
- Hospitality and Catering
- Leisure and Tourism
- Media Studies

- Manufacturing
- Modern foreign languages
- Music
- Physical Education

The work through controlled assessment contributes towards the final grade so it is very important.

Employers regard GCSEs as a key factor when looking at young people they might take on for jobs or training. A large survey of employers found that 15% of employers ignored **CVs** if the job applicant did not have five good GCSEs (usually meaning five at grades A*–C). On average, employers said they would pay someone a 17% higher starting salary if they had five good GCSEs.

Are GCSEs a lot of work?

Yes. GCSE courses – and other courses that run in Key Stage 4 – are demanding. You will need to make a sustained and consistent effort, usually over a 2-year period. And you can expect to have 1 or 2 hours per week homework in each of your subjects or courses.

Applied GCSEs

Applied GCSEs each relate to a particular area of work. They are available in the following subjects:

- Applied Art and Design
- Applied Business
- Applied Information and Communication Technology
- Applied Science
- Engineering
- Health and Social Care
- Leisure and Tourism
- Manufacturing.

Applied GCSEs are assessed at the same standard as other GCSEs, although the work you produce will tend to be more practical. In Applied GCSEs, the focus is mainly on controlled assessment. You will carry out your own investigations and produce a **portfolio** of work, but you will still have to take some tests or exams. The qualification is made up of three units of equal value. Normally, two-thirds of your work is assessed by your teachers, and one-third by external examiners. As with other GCSEs, Applied GCSEs are graded A*–G, but each Applied GCSE is equal to two GCSEs.

If you are at school, your lessons for taking an Applied GCSE may take place in a local college or at a **vocational** learning centre.

Short course GCSEs

The short course GCSE is designed to take only half the study time of a full GCSE. The short course can be taught over 1 or 2 years.

GCSE short courses require you to do controlled assessments and exams to the same standards as a full GCSE, but they cover only half the content. GCSE short courses are graded A*–G, and each one counts as half a GCSE. Employers and colleges of further education (**FE**) understand that GCSE short courses are equal to half a GCSE, so that, if you do two short courses, you will have the equivalent of one GCSE.

GCSE short courses are available in:

- Ancient History
- Citizenship Studies
- Classical Civilisation
- Design and Technology
- Geography
- History
- Latin
- Modern foreign languages (Dutch, French, German, Gujarati, Persian, Portuguese, Spanish and Turkish)
- Physical Education
- Religious Studies
- Welsh as a Second Language

Short course GCSEs can be used in different ways. For example:

- they can help you to take more subjects, such as a second modern foreign language
- if other subject choices prevent you from taking a full GCSE, you can still gain a short-course qualification in subjects such as Art and Design, Geography, ICT, PE or Religious Education (remember that RE and PE are compulsory subjects, though not necessarily requiring an exam qualification)
- if you need extra time to develop, you can do a short course GCSE in the time taken by a full GCSE course.

But remember that short courses aren't an easy option. Even though they are meant to take up just half the time, they can end up taking more than that.

When will I start my GCSEs and other Key Stage 4 options? ?

GCSE courses usually start at the beginning of Year 10 and take 2 years to complete. But this is not an absolute rule. Some schools begin a few, or even all, of their Key Stage 4 courses a year earlier, that is, at the beginning of Year 9. This rarely happens with the Diplomas. This is because they were designed for the 14–19 age group.

Diplomas

Diplomas are new qualifications that are offered to the 14–19 age group, including Key Stage 4. Many local 14–19 **partnerships or consortia** are now offering some Diploma courses.

The Diplomas provide an alternative to more traditional education and qualifications. They have been developed by employers, schools, colleges and universities. The aim is to help young people realise their potential and gain knowledge and skills in a 'real world' environment.

Each Diploma is intended to give you the right knowledge and experience to prepare you for the next stage in your learning or career pathway – at school, college, university or work.

For young people at Key Stage 4, the Diploma option will normally be at Level 1 or Level 2. You can select whichever level Diploma suits you best.

- Level 1 (Foundation level): equivalent in size and status to four to five GCSEs at grades D–G
- Level 2 (Higher level): equivalent in size and status to five to six GCSEs at grades A*–C.

From September 2010, Diploma courses will be available in 14 subject areas:

- Business, Administration and Finance
- Construction and the Built Environment
- Creative and Media
- Engineering
- Environmental and Land-based Studies
- Hair and Beauty Studies
- Hospitality
- Information Technology
- Manufacturing and Product Design
- Public Services
- Retail Business
- Society, Health and Development
- Sport and Active Leisure
- Travel and Tourism.

What's good about the Diplomas?

Local partnerships or consortia have had to apply for the right to run these Diploma courses. In each subject or 'learning line' the partnerships work with employers to give young people options that combine practical and academic learning, alongside other qualifications such as GCSEs, **A levels** and Apprenticeships. You can learn in different environments, including schools, colleges and the workplace. The Diploma qualifications are intended to help you to progress towards skilled jobs as well as further education.

Three more areas are due to become available in 2011:

- Humanities and Social Sciences
- Languages and International Communication
- Science.

All Diploma students take on further study in English, Maths and IT. You will also need to develop your Personal Learning and Thinking Skills. See page 15 for more on these and other skills.

Each Diploma includes a project that will help you develop your ability to work independently. You will also have at least 10 days' work experience. Because employers are involved in the design and delivery of the Diplomas, the qualification is valued by employers. The Higher level Diplomas are also acceptable for applying to university.

> **?**
>
> # Would a Diploma suit me if I am a more practical sort of person?
>
> Diplomas are not all out practical courses. They combine theoretical learning with a more 'hands-on', practical approach. For example, there is quite a lot of opportunity for **work-based learning** that includes spending a considerable period of time in the workplace. Diplomas provide a broad introduction to a particular **occupational area**, rather than specific training in that area. BTEC Diplomas, OCR Nationals and NVQs (when available in schools) are closer to a practical, vocational approach, with rather less emphasis on academic learning.

Entry level qualifications

Entry level is the first tier on the National Qualifications and Credit Framework and Entry level qualifications are nationally recognised qualifications. They measure achievement below GCSE grade G and Level 1 on the National Qualifications Framework (**NQF**). These qualifications are meant for students who may not be ready yet to take a GCSE qualification in one or more subjects. Work in these courses is taken at a slower pace and there is plenty of opportunity to make good any gaps in your existing knowledge and understanding. The approach is more practical and you will develop the ability to apply your learning in everyday situations. So, taking these qualifications should help you build your basic knowledge and skills,

For further information on Entry level qualifications, turn to page 143.

Vocational courses

Vocational courses put even more emphasis on preparation for working life. They are an important option if you feel ready to start to prepare for working life, perhaps by learning about a particular career sector. Some of the courses are more specific and help you acquire particular skills needed to do a particular job. A lot of the work is practical and it may include some time away from the school, in a workplace, a further education college or learning centre.

For further information on vocational courses, turn to page 133.

It is difficult for most schools to provide a full range of vocational courses. Many schools are now working with other partners, particularly further education colleges, to provide a range of vocational learning programmes. These programmes allow some Key Stage 4 students to follow courses that are not available at their own school. The courses lead to vocational qualifications, such as GCSEs in vocational subjects or NVQs. Check with your school to find out what vocational options are available for you.

BTEC (Business Technology and Education Council) qualifications

BTEC qualifications are most commonly found in post-16 and adult education, but also make a strong contribution to Key Stage 4. They are work-related qualifications, available in a wide range of subjects, including:

- Applied Science
- Art and Design
- Business
- Construction
- E-business
- Engineering
- Health and Social Care
- Hospitality
- IT
- Land and Environment
- Media
- Performing Arts
- Public Services
- Retail
- Sport
- Travel and Tourism.

You can take a BTEC qualification if you are interested in learning more about a particular sector or industry.

Employers have helped design the BTEC qualifications, so that they give you the skills and knowledge that employers want.

You can take BTECs either as a way of preparing for direct entry to work or as a step towards continued study at the next level – in a school, college or a more specialist vocational area.

The qualifications offer a mix of theory and practice, and often include work experience. They can take the form of (or be part of) a **technical certificate**. They form one of the key elements of an Apprenticeship.

BTEC qualifications range from Entry level to Level 8 on the National Qualifications Framework. However, most qualifications in Key Stage 4 fit in at Entry level, Level 1 or Level 2 (see the chart on page 20 for further details).

> # Would a BTEC qualification suit me?
>
> **?**
>
> If you clearly know that you wish to work in a particular area a BTEC might suit you. For example, the BTEC First in Horticulture is a vocational course that might suit you if you are interested in horticulture and if you prefer a practical learning approach. The three units studied are:
>
> - commercial horticulture crop production
> - land-based machinery operation
> - practical land-based skills.
>
> After doing such a course, if you still feel enthusiastic about the study area, you could continue on to take a more demanding Level 3 qualification, such as the BTEC National.

BTEC Assessment

While studying for a BTEC, you have to complete a range of assignments, case studies and practical activities. You also produce a portfolio that shows the work you have completed. BTEC qualifications are graded pass, merit or distinction.

See page 134 for further information on BTEC qualifications.

OCR Nationals

OCR Nationals are also work-related qualifications. Like BTEC courses, they are most commonly found in post-16 and adult education, but they also appear at Key Stage 4. They are available in the following subjects:

- Art and Design
- Health and Social Care
- ICT
- Media
- Public Services
- Science
- Sport
- Travel and Tourism.

OCR Nationals provide a practical approach to learning. You can take an OCR National if you are interested in learning more about a particular career sector or industry. As with the BTECs, many have been designed in collaboration with employers. They can be taken either as a way of preparing for entry to work or as a step towards continued study at the next level.

OCR Nationals are available at Levels 1–3, but it is Levels 1 and 2 that are most commonly found in Key Stage 4 (see the chart on page 20 for further details). At Level 2, for example, you will be given help to perform a variety of tasks with some guidance or supervision.

How would I be assessed?

You will be assessed by your teacher but sometimes also by an external examiner. You complete a range of assignments, case studies and practical activities, as well as a portfolio of evidence. OCR Nationals are graded Pass, Merit or Distinction.

See page 138 for further information on OCR Nationals.

City & Guilds qualifications

City & Guilds is another exam board that provides a wide range of courses, through all National Qualifications Framework levels (see Jargon Buster box on page 19). The qualifications are mostly vocational, but City & Guilds also offers courses in, for example, literacy, numeracy and IT. These are sometimes available in schools, but more often the courses are available in colleges and the workplace, or in preparation for employment.

See page 136 for further information on City & Guilds qualifications.

Young Apprenticeships

Young Apprenticeships at Key Stage 4 provide another way of combining continued school study with a taste of real work at college, with a **training provider** and/or in the workplace. The Young Apprenticeship programme is aimed at able and motivated students who want a more practical style of learning.

Young Apprenticeships may be available in your area in subjects such as:

- Art and Design
- Business Administration
- Construction
- Engineering
- Food and Drink Manufacturing
- Hairdressing
- Health and Social Care
- Hospitality
- Motor Industry
- Performing Arts

- Retail
- Science and the Electricity Industry
- Sports Management, Leadership and Coaching
- Textiles.

You study the normal curriculum at school, including English, Mathematics, ICT and Science. You also spend around 2 days a week working towards NVQs or other nationally recognised vocational qualifications. This time may be spent at a college of further education, although some schools do provide this part of the programme. You will also spend up to 50 days over 2 years gaining experience with an employer, training company or college (or a combination of two or three of these).

After completing a Young Apprenticeship you can choose to continue in education and training, or you can go on to do a full-time Apprenticeship in the same sector area. (If you have completed the Young Apprenticeships programme you may be able to move more quickly towards completion of a full-time Apprenticeship in your chosen area.)

ASDAN

The Award Scheme Development and Accreditation Network (ASDAN) is a **curriculum development organisation**. ASDAN offers a wide range of curriculum programmes and qualifications for all abilities, mainly in the 11–25 age group.

ASDAN programmes and qualifications run at many different levels, from Entry level to university entrance. They are activity-based programmes that reward learners for their success in developing a range of skills, including Key Skills and other personal and social skills.

Students on ASDAN programmes can gain Bronze, Silver, Gold and Universities Awards. These are progressive awards and the highest level (the Universities Award) attracts 70 points in the **UCAS** Tariff (see page 17).

ASDAN programmes that are run in schools include:

- Certificate of Personal Effectiveness (**CoPE**): this runs at Levels 1, 2 and 3. It links to the various levels of award that are central to the overall ASDAN programme.
- Key Skills Qualifications: improving own learning, working with others, problem solving.
- Certificate in Career Planning: offered at Levels 1–3, this supports the development and accreditation of careers-related education and guidance at both Key Stage 4 and post-16.
- Certificate in Life Skills: a unit-based qualification that offers accreditation at Entry 1, 2 and 3.

NVQs (National Vocational Qualifications)

The list of NVQs is almost endless; those available in some schools or school–college partnerships include:

What are NVQs?

NVQs are work-related qualifications that focus on the practical skills and knowledge needed to do a job. They are far more common post-16 and adult training, for example as part of an Apprenticeship. However, in some cases you can also do an NVQ while you are still at school.

- Agriculture
- Beauty Therapy
- Clinical Laboratory Support
- Learning, Development and Support Services
- Management
- Retail
- Sport and Recreation.

See page 137 for further information on NVQs.

Other vocational qualifications

There are many other vocational courses that schools or colleges offer outside the above categories. Some of them take the form of 'taster' courses, providing a basic introduction to an occupational sector. These do not usually lead to a formal qualification. Others, such as a **CACHE** qualification, may be studied for as long as the major GCSE subjects, but they are still only one part of the broader study programme.

See page 142 for further information on other vocational qualifications.

Key Skills, Functional Skills, and Personal Learning and Thinking Skills

Until 2010, Key Skills is the term that is being used to cover a broad range of skills. From 2010 onwards, skills programmes will increasingly be delivered as Functional Skills or as Personal Learning and Thinking Skills (PLTS).

Jargon Buster: Key Skills

Whatever subjects or courses you are taking, you also need the skills to help you when you start to look for work – and in life more generally. Key Skills are transferable skills, that is, you can use the same skills in different situations. They are skills that employers see as essential in people they are recruiting.

The main three Key Skills are:

- application of number
- communication
- information and communication technology.

There are also three 'wider' Key Skills:

- improving own learning and performance
- problem solving
- working with others.

You will study and develop these Key Skills at school or college, often as part of another course (see also Functional Skills, page 17). Of course, you can also develop the Key Skills outside the classroom, e.g. in a Duke of Edinburgh's Award scheme or through involvement in a club or sporting activity. Later on, after leaving school, you may find that you can take Key Skills qualifications through an employer or training providers. For example, Key Skills are also included in an Apprenticeship. They also form part of some higher education courses.

Key Skills qualifications can have several useful purposes.

- They give you firm evidence of what you have achieved in your learning programme.
- They help build your confidence in your own abilities.
- They support your CV and show employers what you can do.
- They help you move on to further qualifications, including higher education (see 'UCAS points' below).

How Key Skills are taught and assessed

Key Skills are available at Levels 1–4 of the National Qualifications Framework and there are no minimum entry requirements. You can study them alongside other types of qualifications, such as GCSEs, but you do not necessarily take the qualification at the same level as your other qualifications: you take them at whichever level best suits you.

Each Key Skill is assessed separately. The assessment is based on a portfolio you produce and this is assessed internally by your school, college or trainer.

For the three main Key Skills, you also take a test, which is marked externally by an awarding body. At Levels 1 and 2, the test consists of 40 multiple choice questions, each with four possible answers. If you don't pass the test, generally you can retake it as many times as you want, however, you need to check these arrangements with your school, college or learning provider.

Test how good your Key Skills are

You can take a practice test online for the three main Key Skills qualifications at the Key Skills website: www.keyskills4u.com.

Functional Skills

Functional Skills are practical skills in English, Mathematics and ICT. They are a new set of qualifications, launching in 2010. They will be available for all learners aged 14 and above (although it will be possible to take them at a younger age too).

Functional Skills are not just about gaining knowledge in English, Mathematics and ICT. They are also about knowing when and how to use the knowledge in real-life situations. They are intended to help you to communicate more effectively and to be more literate (that is, having a good understanding of the subject). They help you to make sense of your community and the wider world and to develop your own perspectives (that is, your own thinking and evaluation of a particular situation). With good Functional Skills, you should also be able to respond positively to changes in technology and everyday life, that is you should not feel hampered in things that you do.

How Functional Skills are assessed
The main assessment will be completing a set of practical tasks within a given time limit. These tasks will allow you to apply your knowledge, skills and understanding in real-life contexts. The awarding bodies that are developing Functional Skills are also looking at new ways to assess learners, such as electronic and online methods.

Personal Learning and Thinking Skills

There is also a wider framework of six groups of skills that, together with the Functional Skills of English, Mathematics and ICT, are essential to success in learning, life and work.

Are these qualifications going to be a lot of work?

Yes, but it is spread over 2 years. If you are concerned about the balance of learning (the amount of time you will spend on acquiring knowledge and understanding, as against the time you will spend on actually doing things and learning skills), you should talk about it to your teachers.

Key Stage 4 and UCAS points

How to find out more about each type of qualification

- All 14–19 qualifications: www.direct.gov.uk/en/EducationAndLearning/ QualificationsExplained.
- Apprenticeships (including Young Apprenticeships): www.apprenticeships.org.uk.
- BTECs, OCR Nationals and other vocational qualifications: www.direct.gov.uk/en/ EducationAndLearning/QualificationsExplained/DG_10039020.

Jargon Buster: UCAS

!

UCAS is the Universities Central Admissions Scheme and the Tariff is the UCAS system for allocating points to qualifications used for entry to higher education.

It allows students to use a range of different qualifications to help gain a place on an undergraduate course, although other factors are also taken into account when considering applications.

The Tariff is mostly concerned with post-16 qualifications, such as A levels, BTEC Nationals and Scottish Highers. But points are also allocated for some qualifications that can be taken during Key Stage 4, e.g. Key Skills (at Levels 2–4). Full details of the UCAS Tariff are available at www.ucas.com/students/ucas_tariff

- Diplomas: http://yp.direct.gov.uk/diplomas.
- Functional Skills: www.direct.gov.uk/en/EducationAndLearning/ QualificationsExplained/DG_173874
- GCSEs, Applied GCSEs and Short GCSEs: see Part Two of this book.
- Key Skills: www.keyskills4u.com.

By now you should have an idea of some of the most common Key Stage 4 options. But how do you decide between them? The following pages will help.

CHAPTER TWO

Choosing your qualification

In this chapter you will:

- *get help with choosing the right Key Stage 4 qualifications*
- *find out how the different qualifications compare with one another*
- *do a brief exercise to help you choose the right qualifications.*

With so many options available at Key Stage 4, it may all seem rather confusing. So, how do you set about making the best choice? One of the best ways is by comparing qualifications with one another and by focusing on what you think you might do after Key Stage 4.

Let's start by comparing the qualifications with one another.

Jargon Buster: National Qualifications Framework

The National Qualifications Framework (NQF) sets out the levels at which qualifications are recognised. Only qualifications that have been accredited by the regulatory authority are included in the NQF.

One of the reasons for having the NQF is so that you can compare various qualifications more easily. The different qualifications are grouped at nine different levels (Entry level and Levels 1–8). All approved qualifications are allocated to a certain level. This is so that you can compare them easily and you can progress from one level to the next.

Qualifications at the same level in the NQF recognise a similar level of knowledge, skills and understanding, although the subjects studied may be quite different. The higher the level, the more advanced the qualification and the more knowledge and skill it requires.

Look at the chart below to find out how different qualifications compare. You will see, for example, that GCSEs cover the Foundation and Intermediate levels (Levels 1 and 2). Grades D–G are Level 1 and grades A*–C are Level 2. A levels are Level 3 qualifications.

If you are still finding it difficult to decide which is the best set of qualifications for you, the following exercise should help you. Look at the statement on the left-hand side and see if it applies to you. If it does, then look at the corresponding qualification[s] on the right-hand side. Then you can research these particular qualifications further, through this book and elsewhere.

Table 2

Qualification level	What it means	Examples of qualifications at this level
Entry level	Builds a basic level of knowledge, understanding and skills and is not geared towards specific occupations	Entry 1, Entry 2 and Entry 3, in a range of areas including National Curriculum subjects, life skills, basic skills, and skills for working life
Level 1	Basic knowledge, understanding and skills, and the ability to apply learning to everyday situations. In some cases, may include initial preparation for job competence	GCSE grades D–G; ASDAN Level 1 certificates; Key Skills Level 1; VRQ Level 1, e.g. OCR Nationals, BTEC Introductory; NVQ Level 1
Level 2	Basic knowledge and/or skills in relation to subject or sector areas; gaining ability to apply learning to a varied range of tasks. This is normally the minimum level required by employers and is critical to going on to further study and higher level skills	GCSE grades A*–C; Key Skills Level 2, VRQ Level 2, e.g. City & Guilds Progression awards; NVQ Level 2
Level 3	Learning at this level involves obtaining in-depth knowledge, understanding and skills, and a higher level of application. Appropriate for people who want to go to university, or to further training or employment	GCE AS and A levels, Advanced Extension Awards, Key Skills Level 3, VRQ Level 3, e.g. NVQ Level 3
Level 4–8	Specialist learning involving high level of knowledge in a specific occupational role or study. Appropriate for people working or wishing to progress to specialised technical and professional jobs, and/or managing and developing others	Certificates and Diplomas of Higher Education, Bachelor's degrees, Foundation degrees, HNCs and HNDs, Key Skills Level 4, NVQ Levels 4 and 5

Table 3

Does this statement apply to you?	Most appropriate qualification[s]
I want a qualification that will give me practical skills towards a specific job	Young Apprenticeships; NVQs; BTEC qualifications and OCR Nationals. All probably with some GCSEs
I want an academic qualification that will help me go on to A levels (or equivalent)	GCSEs; Applied GCSEs; Diplomas
I want to carry on with full-time study at 16+, but on a course related to a particular sector of work	Diplomas; GCSEs; Applied GCSEs
I think I might struggle to achieve any sort of grades at GCSE	Entry level. But you may be able to mix this with some GCSE study.
I am quite good at academic work, but enjoy practical work more	Applied GCSEs; Diplomas; Young Apprenticeships
I've got so many subjects I want to take and am reluctant to give them all up	GCSEs and short course GCSEs

The next section focuses on choosing between specific subjects, mainly with GCSEs in mind. If you need more specific information on other Key Stage 4 qualifications, look at the relevant websites listed on page 156.

CHAPTER THREE

Choosing your subjects

This chapter includes:

- *answers to the most common questions asked by students*
- *exercises to help you decide between subjects*
- *a breakdown of the GCSE results from summer 2009*
- *sources of further information.*

This chapter looks at the kinds of things to consider when you're trying to choose between different subjects. We'll look at some of the most common questions that young people ask.

Should I choose those subjects I am strongest in?

On the whole, this is as good a reason as any to choose a subject at Key Stage 4. If you are strong in a particular subject that you have already been studying, it is more than likely that you will do well at Key Stage 4. This means that you should achieve a good grade at GCSE (or equivalent). It also keeps open the possibility of higher-level study in these same subjects, at A level and beyond. Remember, though, that it is important to put together a well-balanced programme of study at Key Stage 4. You may even find that it is in your long-term interests to keep up one or more subjects where you do not feel as strong. For example, if you are very good at Biology and have an interest in an eventual career in the biological sciences, you will need to keep up Chemistry (by taking it as a separate GCSE or within GCSE Science); this could apply even if you feel at present that you might struggle to achieve the standard required in Chemistry.

Should I choose those subjects I enjoy the most?

It's possible to be good at a subject and yet not really enjoy it – and the reverse can also be true. However, you do tend to do better in subjects you are really interested in. This is largely because you have a natural talent for that area, and also because you are likely to have the motivation to do the additional study needed to get the top grades.

If you are uncertain what your natural talents are, the following table might help you. Look at the skills on the left-hand side of the table and decide which ones you'd definitely like to use in further study, and those you definitely wouldn't be interested in. Put a tick or a cross in each case. Then look to see which subjects match which skills and whether that sheds any light on where your natural talents lie.

Table 4

Type of skill	I like using this skill	I hate using this skill	Subjects that require this skill a lot
Communication skills – good at communicating, reading, writing essays, learning languages			All subjects, but especially English (compulsory), Health and Social Care, History, social science subjects, Leisure and Tourism, modern foreign languages. Diplomas in Creative and Media; Public Services; Society, Health and Development
Attention to detail – being good with small details, checking facts, figures,"specifics, quantities			All science subjects, as well as Geography, Health and Social Care, History, Construction, Engineering, Manufacturing. Diplomas in Business, Administration and Finance; Construction and the Built Environment; Engineering; Information Technology; Manufacturing and Product Design; Public Services
Physical ability – e.g. making things, doing things, exercising, using your hands, doing experiments			Physical Education, science subjects, Engineering, Art and Design, and Design and Technology, Manufacturing. Diplomas in Construction and the Built Environment; Hair and Beauty; Hospitality; Manufacturing and Product Design; Sport and Active Leisure
Creative ability – e.g. making things, writing or drawing, performing			Art and Design, Design and Technology, English (compulsory) and English Literature, Drama, Performing Arts, Music. Diplomas in Construction and the Built Environment; Creative and Media; Engineering; Manufacturing and Product Design
Memory and recall skills – memorising facts, words, vocabulary and theories			Many subjects, but especially History, Mathematics (compulsory), science subjects, modern foreign languages. Diploma in Business, Administration and Finance; Engineering; Society, Health and Development; Travel and Tourism
IT and computing skills – using hardware, software and systems			ICT (compulsory), Design and Technology, Engineering, Leisure and Tourism, Physics. Diplomas in Business, Administration and Finance; Construction and the Built Environment; Creative and Media; Engineering; Hospitality; Information Technology; Manufacturing and Product Design; Public Services; Society, Health and Development; Travel and Tourism
Mathematical skills – using figures and stats to conclude and investigate things; doing mental calculations			Mathematics (compulsory), all science subjects (especially Physics), Engineering, Design and Technology, Geography. Diplomas in Business, Administration and Finance; Construction and the Built Environment; Engineering; Environmental and Land-based Studies; Manufacturing and Product Design; Retail Business; Travel and Tourism

Continued

Type of skill	I like using this skill	I hate using this skill	Subjects that require this skill a lot
Emotional intelligence skills – empathy, intuition, vision, creativity, tact, interpersonal skills			Religious Studies, English (compulsory) and English Literature, Health and Social Care, History, Leisure and Tourism, Music. Diplomas in Creative and Media; Hair and Beauty Studies; Hospitality; Public Services; Retail Business; Society, Health and Development; Sport and Active Leisure; Travel and Tourism
Spatial awareness and mechanical skills – being able to 'see' what shapes will fit where; making and working with mechanical objects			Engineering, Physics, Art and Design, Design and Technology, ICT (compulsory), Construction. Diplomas in Construction and the Built Environment; Engineering; Manufacturing and Product Design
Business skills – understanding business, finance and economics, as well as specific sectors of work			Business Studies, Leisure and Tourism, Retail. Diplomas in Business, Administration and Finance; Hair and Beauty Studies; Hospitality; Public Services; Retail Business; Travel and Tourism
Citizenship skills – being familiar with and learning about social, political and environmental issues of the past and present			Citizenship (compulsory), Geography, History, Social Science subjects, Religious Studies, English (compulsory) and English Literature. Diplomas in Environmental and Land-based Studies; Public Services; Society, Health and Development; Sport and Active Leisure

How are the different subjects assessed?

Most GCSEs and their equivalents are assessed by a combination of:

- written exams (either during or at the end of your course)
- controlled assessments (essays, projects or case studies completed during the course)
- practical tests or exams.

Not only are there variations between subjects in the type of assessment, but there will also be some variation between different examination boards offering the same subject. So try to work out whether you are better at exams, controlled assessments or practical work, and bear that in mind when choosing your particular subjects.

How can I avoid taking too many exams?

Many of the subjects that you will study in Key Stage 4 will be assessed on a mixture of exams and controlled assessments. Controlled assessment was introduced recently and it means that the assessments have to be supervised effectively if they are going to contribute to the final GCSE grades.

Under the new arrangements, if you are preparing an essay in a particular subject, you might carry out the research for it outside the classroom, but you would write the essay itself under controlled supervised conditions.

Controlled assessments are a useful way of showing what you can do, especially when an exam is not appropriate (for example, a music presentation). The controlled assessment element can make up a significant proportion of your final mark – for some subjects, controlled assessments count for more than half of the total. The detailed entries for each subject in Part Two will give you some idea of the assessment weighting – how many of the marks are given for controlled assessment and how many for the examination component.

However, even if you do prefer controlled assessment to exams, try to avoid assignment overload. Some subjects involve doing more research outside the classroom. History and Geography are examples of this. Mathematics and modern foreign languages, on the other hand, will probably include relatively little outside research. As it's important to have sufficient time to do every project well, make sure you get the workload right by *not* picking too many subjects that are heavy on controlled assessment. So, check controlled assessment weightings with your teachers.

So you will be doing some controlled assessments throughout your GCSE studies. It will be up to your teachers and their organisation of teaching and learning as to when exactly you do the controlled assessment work. Since the assessment counts towards final grades, you need to take it seriously and do it as well as you can. Try to be well organised and don't leave assignments until the last minute.

Within the individual subject, it is unlikely that you will have any freedom of choice. It is your school that chooses a **syllabus** from one of the exam boards for each subject. This means that you could be following different exam boards for different subjects – this is ok; the most important thing is that you know what work you will be covering in your particular syllabus. Your teacher can tell you this, or you can find it on the relevant exam board website.

What are modular courses?

Many courses now have 'modular' options. A modular course is split into different units, with a test or exam at the end of each unit. This means that you sit exams throughout your course instead of doing all the exams at the end of the course. It gives you the opportunity to study relatively small parts of the curriculum in a concentrated period. Each unit or module contains very specific and easily understood learning targets, and learning is assessed at the end of each module.

The different structure of modular courses, which includes an emphasis on assessment and regular feedback between your teacher and you, suits some students better than the more traditional structure. Also, if you take a modular exam and don't do as well as you expected, you can re-sit the module (once only) to try to improve your grade. The better mark from the two sittings will count towards your final GCSE grade. But remember this is not an easy way out and you would still need to work hard towards your first attempt. You would also need to talk to your teachers about the arrangements for re-sitting modules, as these vary, depending on the particular course you are studying.

Which subjects are necessary if I want to go on to higher education?

Although university may seem a long way off at this stage, there are some choices you make now which could influence the range of courses open to you from age 18.

Which university courses look at the GCSEs I have?

English
Some English Literature departments still insist on, or at least prefer, at least one modern foreign language GCSE.

Foreign languages
To study a modern foreign language at university, it is an advantage to have studied at least two foreign languages to GCSE level and, if at all possible, beyond.

Dentistry, Medicine and Veterinary Science
For degree courses in Dentistry, Medicine and Veterinary Science, you should think seriously about taking all three science subjects separately, or at least GCSE Science *and* GCSE Additional Science.

The problem is that the subjects you need will clearly depend on what you will eventually choose to study at university – but you may well not yet know which subject you will want to read at that stage. Usually, it is expected that you have an A level or equivalent with a good grade in that subject; and this very often (but not always) means that you should have taken a GCSE in that same subject.

Do I need to study a particular GCSE or Diploma in a subject to do it at A level or in an Advanced Diploma?

Not necessarily. If you can convince your sixth form tutors or teachers that you have the right attitude and the potential to do well, then it may be possible to go ahead without the previous study. However, there are clearly some subjects that really do build on the knowledge that you will have acquired at Key Stage 4.

You will need Key Stage 4 qualifications in the following subjects to study them at A level:

- Geography
- Mathematics
- modern foreign languages
- the sciences.

It would be difficult to pick these subjects up at A level without any of the building blocks.

There are, however, subjects that are often not taught or studied in a secondary school at GCSE level. Therefore most people meet these subjects for the first time at A level, and for these no prior knowledge is required. These subjects include:

- Government and Politics
- Law
- Philosophy
- Sociology.

The present range of Advanced Diplomas do not require previous study in the same learning line at Foundation or Higher Level Diploma. What will be necessary will be a good general education, with some evidence of good learning ability in particularly relevant subjects, for example:

- English – for Creative and Media; Public Services; Society, Health and Development
- ICT – for the Diplomas in Construction and the Built Environment; Creative and Media; Engineering; Manufacturing and Product Design
- Maths – for the Advanced Diplomas in Business, Administration and Finance; Construction and the Built Environment; Engineering
- Science – for Construction and the Built Environment; Engineering; Environmental and Land-based Studies; Society, Health and Development; Sport and Active Leisure.

How do I make sure that my choice of subjects will be in line with my hopes for a career?

Even if you think you know what sort of job or career pathway you want, you should be prepared to research your job ideas more generally and find out which qualifications you will need. You can do this at your school's Connexions or careers resource centre or library, or at your local Connexions or careers centre (your careers teacher will be able to tell you where this is).

Try to identify something like the full range of skills and abilities needed in that particular occupation. Just to take one example, hairdressing may be an attractive career because

Help! I don't know what to choose

If you've no idea at this stage, don't worry. You are probably in the majority... 13 or 14 is rather early for most people to decide on a career. Your aim now should be to choose a selection of subjects that will keep as many career doors open as possible. There are a few ideas on types of job that link with particular subjects towards the end of each subject entry in Part Two.

you like the idea helping people to make the best of their physical appearance, and you know you like the working environment of a salon or barber's shop. But what about the physical and the business and **enterprise skills** that you would need to set up your own hairdressing business?

Which GCSEs are easiest to get good grades in?

This depends on what you are best at and what you enjoy – that's probably how you will get the best grades.

The top 20 subjects for the highest grades in summer 2009 are given below. Be careful, though: do not use the table as an indication of the level of difficulty of a subject and base your choice on that, as there will be many reasons why a subject gains more top grades than another. In many of these top 20 subjects, it is 'high flyer' students who account for a large percentage of the entries.

Table 5
The Top 20 for summer 2009 GCSEs: subjects with the highest percentage of A* and A grades

	Subject	%
1	Classical Subjects	60.0
2	Other modern foreign languages*	58.8
3	Chemistry	50.9
4	Physics	49.3
5	Biology	47.9
6	Irish	45.2
7	Spanish	34.6
8	Religious Studies	32.7
9	Music	31.0
10	History	30.4
11	Geography	27.1
12	Economics	26.5
13=	French	26.3
13=	ICT	26.3
15	Welsh as Second Language	26.0
16	German	25.0
17	Art	24.0
18	Mathematics (Additional)	23.9
19	PE	23.3
20	Drama	23.1

*Other than French, German and Spanish
Note: the average across all subjects for those achieving A* or A grades was 21.6%.

How can I find out more?

You will almost certainly need more information and help than this book can give you in making your choices. It's worth remembering that there are many sources of help, including the ones listed below.

- *Careers advisers or personal advisers.* If you need additional help to decide on your subject choices, or want to talk about your career options, you can ask for an interview with a careers or personal adviser. These people may not always know you well, but they have a lot of knowledge about the world of work and the importance of the different qualifications to the range of jobs and careers. They may organise group talks in your school about particular careers or topics related to careers. Your careers adviser or personal adviser is also likely to be present at parents' evenings and special careers events that relate to Key Stage 4 choices in your school.
- *Your work experience.* Any work experience placement that you take on during Key Stage 4 will give you a taste of the world of work. Even if you are not trying out the sort of career that is of direct interest to you, you will pick up plenty of experience that will help you see where Key Stage 4 choices fit into the business of setting up a career pathway for yourself.
- *School careers or Connexions library.* Your school will have a careers or Connexions library with details on careers, courses and subjects: it may be located within the main school library. You should explore the full range of books, leaflets and careers software available in your school.
- *Careers or Connexions centre.* There will also be a more extensive careers library at your local careers or Connexions centre. These centres are usually located in or near town centres and are open Monday to Friday, including the school holidays. Your careers teacher or coordinator will be able to tell you where your nearest centre is and you will be welcome to call in.
- Careers software programs, including **Fast Tomato** and **Kudos**.
- Open days at colleges or training providers.
- Careers teacher or coordinator.
- Tutors.
- Subject teachers.

With this information, you should be well placed to begin to make your subject decisions.

Useful websites

Although the Internet can't replace the value of face-to-face guidance from someone who can respond to your needs and questions, it's a fantastic source of information – for both course information and careers information.

The **QCDA** has a dedicated 14–19 learning website, at www.qcda.gov.uk/20891.aspx. As well as giving support and guidance to schools and colleges in managing the whole 14–19

What to think about when choosing your subjects

- How much reading is involved?
- How much writing is involved?
- How much controlled assessment is involved?
- What percentage of the marks is given for controlled assessment?
- Is there the option of different tiers of assessment (see page 82)?
- Is there an oral test?
- Will you have to gather information for yourself?
- Are projects involved?
- What practical skills are involved?
- How much laboratory or fieldwork is involved?

phase of education, it aims to help students get the best from their experience of this stage of education. There are special sections of the website for learners and their parents.

Other relevant websites:

- Careers Service Northern Ireland: www.careersserviceni.com/Cultures/en-GB/ FindAJob/GeneralInfo/Choosing+GCSE+subjects+or+other+courses.htm
- **Careers Wales**: www.careerswales.com/year9
- Connexions Direct: www.connexions-direct.com

By now you should have plenty of information about what to consider when choosing your subjects. Once you've come up with a shortlist, go to Part Two to look at the relevant subjects in detail. This should confirm your choice, or it may make you reconsider. Either way, it's essential information to have before you make your final decision.

PART TWO

DIRECTORY OF GCSEs, DIPLOMAS, VOCATIONAL AND OTHER COURSES AVAILABLE 14–16

CHAPTER FOUR

GCSEs and Applied GCSEs

First a reminder that the main options awailable at Key Stage 4 are:

- *GCSEs*
- *Diplomas*
- *Vocational courses*
- *Entry level qualifications.*

In this section we'll look in greater depth at each of these main options.

What subjects are available at GCSE?

Table 6

Subjects available at Key Stage 4	
Accounting	Classical Civilisation
Additional Mathematics	Dance
Ancient Greek	Design and Technology
Applied Art and Design	Drama
Applied Business	Dutch
Applied Information and Communication Technology	Economics
Applied Science	Electronics
Arabic	Engineering
Art and Design	Engineering and Manufacturing
Astronomy	Environmental Science
Bengali	Film Studies
Biblical Hebrew	Expressive Arts
Buddhism	Food Technology
Business and Communication Systems	French
Business Studies	General Studies
Catering	Geography
Ceramics	Geology
Chinese (Cantonese or Mandarin)	German
Citizenship	Greek (Modern)

Continued

Gujarati	Panjabi (Punjabi)
Health and Social Care	Performing Arts: Dance
Hebrew (Modern)	Persian
Hindi	Philosophy and Ethics
Hinduism	Photography
History	Physical Education
Home Economics	Polish
Human Biology	Portuguese
Human Physiology and Health	Psychology
Humanities	Religious Studies
Indonesian	Rural and Agricultural Science
Information and Communication Technology	Russian
Irish	Sikhism
Islamic Studies	Social Science
Italian	Sociology
Japanese	Spanish
Judaism	Sports Studies
Latin	Statistics
Law	Thai
Leisure and Tourism	Travel and Tourism
Maltese	Turkish
Manufacturing	Urdu
Media Studies	Vietnamese
Moving Image Arts	Welsh
Music	

Note: Some of these subjects are not often available at Key Stage 4. They are likely to be available in further education colleges or other specialist settings.

Directory of GCSEs

The following pages give more detailed information on a range of GCSE subjects that are taken by students at Key Stage 4.

Each subject is covered under the following sections:

- overview of the subject area
- main elements of the course
- applied courses, short courses or other variations available
- how the subject is taught and assessed
- the subject at A level (or equivalent)
- the subject and choosing a career pathway.

Syllabus information

If you need more information on any subject that interests you, it's a good idea to check out the syllabus of the relevant exam board that your school or college follows. These can be found on the exam board websites listed on page 156.

AS/A levels and equivalents

A levels remain the main progression route for those wanting to go on to university and/ or high status careers. There are some excellent alternatives, such as the International Baccalaureate ((**IB**) offered by some schools and sixth form colleges) and BTEC and OCR Nationals (usually offered in colleges of further education).

The availability of courses in the subject area at A level and BTEC National is listed in each subject section.

Future careers

Each subject area includes ideas for possible future careers.

What to do next

As you browse through the subject entries, try to think about the following questions.

* Would I enjoy studying this subject?
* Would I do well in the subject, given the type of assessment methods used?
* How would choosing this subject affect my plans for further study ay 16+?
* How would choosing this subject affect my career options?

Then come up with a shortlist of subjects, and if you are still finding it difficult to choose between a few subjects, go back to Chapter 3, 'Choosing your subjects', in Part One (page 23).

ART AND DESIGN

This subject gives students the opportunities to develop:

- creative and imaginative powers, and the practical skills for communicating and expressing ideas, feelings and meanings in art, craft and design
- investigative, analytical, experimental and interpretative capabilities, aesthetic understanding and **critical skills**
- understanding of codes and conventions of art, craft and design and awareness of contexts in which they operate
- knowledge and understanding of art, craft and design in contemporary societies and in other times and cultures.

GCSE Art and Design

GCSE Art and Design can be an attractive option if you have good basic drawing skills and are interested in developing your visual appreciation of the world around you. This course will introduce you to a wide range of art media and you will have the opportunity to develop your creative capacities in these media.

Main elements of the course

The outline below is based on what the majority of exam board syllabuses include. For an exact description of the syllabus you will be studying, you will need to contact your school or the exam board itself.

The course includes a mix of critical, practical and theoretical study of drawing, painting and other media (this may include ceramics, collage, photography, printmaking, sculpture and mixed media). You will also get some first-hand experience of original work. You will be expected to develop knowledge and understanding of:

- how ideas, feelings and meanings are conveyed in images and artefacts (other artistic objects made by humans)
- a range of art, craft and design processes in two and/or three dimensions (if you are in Northern Ireland, you will cover work in both two and three dimensions), including, where appropriate, the use of computers and ICT
- how images and artefacts relate to their social, historical and cultural context
- a variety of approaches, methods and intentions and the contribution of contemporary practitioners of art and others from different times and cultures to continuity and change in art, craft and design.

Some schools also offer specialist options within Art and Design, such as critical and contextual studies, fine art, graphic design, photography, textiles, or three-dimensional design. Each of these courses can be run at full GCSE level, i.e. as a single GCSE in its own right.

GCSE Applied Art and Design

Applied Art and Design is equivalent to two GCSEs and is normally allocated twice the time given to a single GCSE, so it will probably take up two of the 'option blocks'. This makes it even more important that you have good basic drawing skills and are well motivated in your study of the subject.

The course is made up of three units of work – two-dimensional and three-dimensional visual language; materials, techniques and technology; and working to project briefs.

How is Art and Design taught and assessed?

Art and Design is one of the subject areas where there is a strong practical focus, alongside the 'academic' elements (which include detailed study of particular artists and their work). You will learn how to critically appraise your own work and that of professional artists. You will also learn how to record your observations, experiences and ideas. You will develop and explore ideas and learn how to present a personal response to the range of stimuli that art, craft and design media provide. Most schools ensure that you have the opportunity to visit art galleries and exhibitions and meet professional artists, sometimes working with 'artists in residence'.

You will have to do controlled assessments, as well as an exam.

- Controlled assessment accounts for 60% and the examination 40% of the GCSE course.
- The Applied GCSE course comprises two-thirds controlled assessment and one-third examination.

You will need to build up a portfolio (usually in the form of a sketchbook, but with the frequent inclusion of larger pieces of work). The portfolio will be based on one or more projects (the number depends on the individual exam board). Your teacher will select the unit topics you will study, but each will be aimed at developing your skills, imagination and confidence. The assignments are done both in the classroom and through homework.

For the final project, taken in the final term of Year 11, you will have a set period of time to do your research and thinking and a period of 10 hours (spread over 2 or more days) under exam conditions to complete the piece of work.

Art and Design at A level

A level courses are available in Art and Design and in Applied Art and Design. These courses have painting and drawing as their main focus. However, there are many other topics included the course, such as:

- fashion and textiles
- fine art
- graphic design
- photography and multimedia
- three-dimensional design.

Art and Design and choosing a career

Job opportunities at age 16 are relatively limited in this area of work, but the 14–19 learning stage gives young people interested in art and design the opportunities to experiment with, and develop, their abilities across a spectrum of art and design activity. This is often a narrowing-down process, with the option to specialise as you progress. You can explore **work-based training** (Apprenticeships in England, Modern Apprenticeships in Wales, or Skillseekers and Modern Apprenticeships in Scotland). Alternatively, you can stay on at school or college, to do a Diploma in Creative and Media, A level Art and Design, City & Guilds or BTEC qualifications in Art and Design, or a related area such as Ceramics, Photography or Textiles.

Not all Art and Design graduates enter careers in which they make direct use of their artistic ability and training. Perhaps only a quarter end up working as artists or designers and the proportion is lower still when one looks at those who stay with fine art studies. One growth area in recent years has been in website design, with some scope for creative and imaginative artists and designers with good information technology competence. There are vacancies for graphic design graduates in advertising, the leisure industry, publishing and design consultancy. Many fashion and textiles graduates find jobs in buying and merchandising or with mass production designers. With many of the three-dimensional options (e.g. jewellery and silversmithing, glass and ceramics), it is often most practical to think in terms of self-employment, with what this will mean in terms of developing business skills and **entrepreneurial skills**.

Further information

- Artcyclopedia   www.artcyclopedia.com
- The Artist's Toolkit   www.artsconnected.org/toolkit
- BBC Arts   www.bbc.co.uk/arts
- BBC GCSE Bitesize   www.bbc.co.uk/schools/gcsebitesize/art
- British Council – Arts   www.britishcouncil.org/arts
- Catalogue of Internet Resources   http://bubl.ac.uk/link/linkbrowse. cfm?menuid=9847; http://bubl.ac.uk/link/d/ designeducation.htm
- Design Council   www.designcouncil.org.uk; www.yourcreativefuture.org.uk
- History of Art   www.besthistorysites.net/arthistory.shtml
- Institute of Conservation   www.icon.org.uk
- National Electronic and Video Archive of the Crafts   www.media.uwe.ac.uk/nevac/
- Caprez, Emma, *Art and Design Uncovered*, Trotman

BIOLOGY

Biology includes the study of topics such as digestion, ecology and ecosystems, evolution, gene technology, microbes and food, plants, photosynthesis, and respiration and breathing.

Note: New specifications for GCSEs in all science subjects will start in September 2012.

GCSE Biology

GCSE Biology is one of three separate science awards (the others are Chemistry and Physics) that together cover the requirements of the Key Stage 4 programme of study. You can also combine the study of these three subjects in a GCSE Science and/or Additional Science course (see separate entry for GCSE Science).

GCSE Biology takes the biology from GCSE Science and the biology from GCSE Additional Science and adds a bit more to form a qualification which is wholly Biology. If you study in a state-maintained school, it will be compulsory for you to do the complete programme of study. So you will do courses in all three separate sciences if you take this pathway.

The main advantage of taking the single sciences separately is that you can keep open a wider range of scientific career routes.

Main elements of the course

The outline below is based on what the majority of exam board syllabuses include. For an exact description of the syllabus you will be studying, you will need to contact your school or the exam board itself.

The main topics in the GCSE Biology course are:

- digestion
- ecology
- ecosystems
- gene technology
- microbes and food
- photosynthesis
- respiration and breathing.

In studying Biology, you will learn about how new knowledge in areas such as ecology, genetics and biodiversity (the study of the various organisms that live together in a particular geographical area) affects our lives and the environment. You will begin to have an understanding of scientific ideas, how they develop, what may affect their development, and their power and limitations. You will plan and carry out several experiments, considering and evaluating data you have collected yourself and that obtained from other sources. You will start to evaluate the benefits and drawbacks of scientific and technological developments, such as those related to the environment, our personal health and quality of life, and consider the **ethical issues** involved. You will also learn how to select, organise and present information clearly and logically, using appropriate scientific terms and rules. The use of ICT has an important role in much of the teaching and learning in Biology.

GCSE Human Physiology and Health

Some schools and colleges offer Human Physiology and Health GCSE as an alternative to Biology. In just the same way as Biology, GCSE in Human Physiology and Health is one of the Key Stage 4 GCSE science subjects that meet the Key Stage 4 Science programme of study.

In this subject you will learn about:

- humans and other organisms
- the skeletal system
- health and hygiene.

How are Biology and Human Physiology and Health taught and assessed?

You will be taught how to:

- recognise, recall and show understanding of specific scientific facts, terms, principles, ideas and practical techniques
- show understanding of the power and limitations of scientific ideas and the things that affect how these ideas develop
- use your knowledge to show understanding of the benefits and drawbacks of applications of science
- apply your knowledge and understanding by analysis and evaluation of information and data
- apply investigative methods (that is, do experiments), including practical techniques that require skill.

The style and weightings of assessment vary between different syllabuses, but each scheme of assessment includes a final exam.

Biology at A level

A level Biology covers areas such as:

- biological foundations
- human health and disease
- key biological concepts
- transport and exchange in mammals and plants.

Students usually need at least a grade C in GCSE Biology or Science to take up A level Biology, as much of the syllabus requires some prior knowledge. Ability in mathematics and chemistry is also useful: students will have to collect and input data, as well as understand the chemical processes that take place in the living world.

Biology and choosing a career

Taking one or more of the separate sciences as a GCSE is the best way of preparing for an A level in the same subject. If you are thinking of a career that is directly related to biology, it is best if you can offer some strength in mathematics and/or the physical sciences – physics and chemistry. With A levels or an equivalent qualification (such as the BTEC Diploma) you could look at work in health care (including nursing), laboratory work, or work in a dental surgery. If you plan to go to university, after graduation the areas of employment directly related to biology that you can look at include animal care, biotechnology, cytogenetics, medical sales, pharmacology, scientific laboratory work and veterinary science.

Further information

- ARKive   www.arkive.org

- Association of the British   www.abpischools.org.uk
  Pharmaceutical Industry (ABPI)

- BBC Science and Nature   www.bbc.co.uk/sn

- Biotopics   www.biotopics.co.uk

- BrainPOP   www.brainpop.com

- Catalogue of Internet Resources: bubl.ac.uk/link/b/biologyeducation.htm

- Institute of Biology   www.societyofbiology.org/education

- Living Library   www.livinglibrary.co.uk

- Making Sense of Health   www.makingsenseofhealth.org.uk

- S-Cool   www.s-cool.co.uk/gcse/biology.html

- Science and plants for schools: www-saps.plantsci.cam.ac.uk

- Sparknotes – Biology   www.sparknotes.com/biology/

BUSINESS STUDIES

A course in business studies and related areas (see variations below) will give you the chance to develop knowledge and understanding of the business world. Learning about how business works will also make you more aware of your own role as a consumer, worker, citizen and, possibly, as a business owner.

GCSE Business Studies

GCSE Business Studies will help you to develop an understanding of:

- the connection between business activity and the changing environment within which the activity takes place
- the contribution that organisations make to wealth creation (this is the process by which a person or an organisation or even a country becomes richer or more successful) and the success of the society in which they work
- the structure, organisation and control of the main forms of business
- the nature and role of enterprise (specific projects aiming specially at growing a business) and business management
- national and international competition
- e-commerce (using electronic ways to do business, for example, using credit cards).

This course will also help you develop your communication, planning and evaluation skills and enable you to use these skills appropriately in the private (e.g. business), public (e.g. local government services) or voluntary (e.g. charities) areas.

Main elements of the course

The outline below is based on what the majority of exam board syllabuses include. For an exact description of the syllabus you will be studying, you will need to contact your school or the exam board itself.

You will be introduced to a range of topics, such as the external environment of a business; business aims, structure, organisation and control; business behaviour; people in a business or organisational environment; aiding and controlling business activity; business communication; finance; marketing; production.

Other GCSE courses offered in this subject area
- Business and Communication Systems
- Business Studies and Economics
- Economics
- Statistics.

GCSE Applied Business (Double Award)

GCSE Applied Business, like Business Studies, includes the study of the business sector. The difference lies mainly in the approach to teaching and learning: Applied Business offers a more practical approach. You will investigate local and/or national business organisations, and employer–employee relationships. The course will help you develop and apply practical, presentational, personal/interpersonal and thinking skills.

The course is composed of the following three units:

- Unit 1 – investigating business
- Unit 2 – people and business
- Unit 3 – business finance.

This qualification is a double award, so is the same value as two GCSEs.

How is Business Studies taught and assessed?

In Business Studies, instead of doing coursework that is teacher set and marked you will do controlled assessments. Assessment consists of 40% examination and 60% controlled assessment. The controlled assessment will probably include a major piece of project work, for example on how to make a business successful through marketing. You will have to demonstrate your ability to apply your knowledge and understanding of the subject content. You will do this by: using appropriate terms, ideas and theories to deal with a given problem; selecting, organising, interpreting and using information from various sources to analyse problems; and evaluating evidence, making reasoned judgements and presenting conclusions accurately, in the context of your project work.

For the Applied Business GCSE, assessment is also composed of 60% controlled assessment and 40% examination, but there will be two controlled assessment projects.

Business Studies at A level

Business Studies A levels are available in Business Studies and Applied Business Studies. The courses are designed to help develop an understanding of business organisations, the markets they serve and the process of adding value. You are also encouraged to view business behaviour from a variety of perspectives by looking into the interests of stakeholders and issues relating to the protection of our environment.

The main elements of the course include:

- analysis and decision-making
- business planning
- business structures, objectives and external influences
- corporate strategy
- financial management
- marketing and production.

The Applied course goes into greater detail on some of the business functions/areas of study. Also, you can take an option with a more specialised vocational focus.

Business Studies and choosing a career

The courses help you to build a foundation of knowledge, understanding and skills that will prepare you for further study or for the world of work. Direct entry is possible at 16, but if you wish you can continue your studies by taking **AS/A2** levels, a BTEC Diploma, NVQ or other course at an equivalent level. These can lead to jobs in, for example, administration, banking, insurance, management, manufacturing, or retail. After graduation, there is a huge range of opportunities, including accountancy, advertising, banking, distribution/logistics, human resources work, law, leisure and tourism, management, marketing, public relations, retail and sales.

Further information

- BBC Business   www.bbc.co.uk/business
- BBC GCSE Bitesize   www.bbc.co.uk/schools/gcsebitesize/business
- Bank of England   www.bankofengland.co.uk
- biz/ed   www.bized.co.uk
- Business Studies Online   www.businessstudiesonline.co.uk
- Council for Administration – Careers   www.breakintobiz
- Investing for Kids   http://library.thinkquest.org/3096
- The Times 100   www.thetimes100.co.uk
- Young Enterprise   www.young-enterprise.org.uk/pub/
- *How to Get Ahead In …Business and Finance*, Raintree

CHEMISTRY

Chemistry is the study of:

- acids and bases
- atomic structure
- bonding
- chemical reactions
- earth materials
- metals
- organic chemicals
- the periodic table
- rates of reaction.

Note: New specifications for GCSEs in all science subjects will start in September 2012.

GCSE Chemistry

GCSE Chemistry is one of three separate science awards (the others are Biology and Physics) that together cover the requirements of the Key Stage 4 programme of study. You can also combine the study of these three subjects in a GCSE Science and/or Additional Science course (see separate entry for GCSE Science).

GCSE Chemistry takes the chemistry from GCSE Science and the chemistry from GCSE Additional Science and adds a bit more to form a qualification which is wholly Chemistry. If you study in a state-maintained school, it will be compulsory for you to do the complete programme of study, so you will be required to follow courses in all three separate sciences if you go down this pathway.

The main advantage of taking the single sciences separately is that you keep open a wider range of scientific career routes.

Main elements of the course

The outline below is based on what the majority of exam board syllabuses include. For an exact description of the syllabus you will be studying, you will need to contact your school or the exam board itself.

The main topics in the GCSE Chemistry course are:

- acids, alkalis and indicators
- atomic structure and bonding
- chemical calculations
- chemical reactions
- electrolysis
- equilibria

- evolution and maintenance of the atmosphere
- extraction of materials
- geological processes
- industrial processes
- particles
- the periodic table.

How is Chemistry taught and assessed?

You will be taught how to:

- recognise, recall and show understanding of specific scientific facts, terms, principles, ideas and practical techniques
- use your understanding of the power and limitations of scientific ideas and the things that affect how these ideas develop
- use your knowledge to show understanding of the benefits and drawbacks of applications of science
- apply your knowledge and understanding by analysis and evaluation of information and data
- apply investigative methods (that is, do experiments), including practical techniques that require skill.

The style and weightings of assessment vary between different syllabuses, but each scheme of assessment has to include a final exam.

Chemistry at A level

The main elements of Chemistry at A level include:

- organic and inorganic chemistry; energetics; kinetics; qualitative equilibria
- laboratory chemistry
- periodicity, quantitative equilibria and functional group chemistry
- transition metals, quantitative kinetics and applied organic chemistry.

Chemistry and choosing a career

Taking one or more of the separate sciences as a GCSE is the best way of preparing for an A level in the same subject. Most jobs using chemistry require high-level qualifications: a degree in Chemistry or a related subject is the most likely entry route for most. Job areas for graduates include analytical chemistry, biochemistry, biomedicine, colour technology, forensic science, industrial research, materials engineering, medical sales, product development, quality assurance, research, scientific journalism, and toxicology.

Further information

- BBC Science and Nature   www.bbc.co.uk/sn

- BrainPOP   www.brainpop.com

- Catalogue of Internet Resources   http://bubl.ac.uk/link/c/chemistryeducation.htm

- Doc Brown's Chemistry Clinic   www.docbrown.info

- GCSE Chemistry   www.gcsescience.com/science-chemistry-enter.htm

- Mr Guch's Cavalcade o'   misterguch.brinkster.net/chemfiestanew.html
  Chemistry:

- Royal Society of Chemistry   www.rsc.org/Education/index.asp

- S-Cool   www.s-cool.co.uk/gcse/chemistry.html

- Sparknotes – Chemistry   www.sparknotes.com/chemistry/

CITIZENSHIP STUDIES

All students in England are required to study Citizenship as a National Curriculum subject. In this course you learn about your rights, responsibilities and duties, and about laws, justice and democracy. Citizenship encourages respect for different national, religious and ethnic identities. You also learn about living in a society and how society has changed and continues to change in the UK, Europe and the wider world.

Citizenship helps you to develop decision-making and critical skills for helping you to deal with political, social, ethical and moral problems. You will also learn how to argue a case on behalf of others as well as yourself and how to speak out on issues of concern and thus be an active member of the British democratic system.

GCSE Citizenship Studies (short course)

Citizenship Studies is only studied as a short course GCSE and counts as half a full GCSE. But many schools use the GCSE qualification as a way of teaching and assessing Citizenship (which is a compulsory subject in Key Stage 4). A GCSE in Citizenship Studies will give you the opportunity to:

- gain knowledge and understanding so that you can become an informed citizen (see subject description above)
- develop skills of enquiry, communication, participation and responsible action
- explore local, national and international issues, problems and events of current interest
- assess your participation within school and/or community activities.

Citizenship Studies can be joined with another short course GCSE to create one full GCSE.

Main elements of the course

The outline below is based on what the majority of exam board syllabuses include. To find out about the exact description of the syllabus you will be studying, you will need to contact your school or the exam board itself.

The GCSE is based on the QCDA **scheme of work** for Citizenship at Key Stage 4. The units of study for the scheme of work are:

- business and enterprise
- challenging racism and discrimination
- consumer rights and responsibilities
- crime – young people and car crime
- Europe – who decides?
- global issues, local action
- how and why laws are made
- how the economy functions
- human rights

- producing the news
- rights and responsibilities in the world of work
- taking part – planning a community event.

How is Citizenship Studies taught and assessed?

In the Citizenship Studies GCSE course, you can expect to take part in:

- group and class discussion on events and issues of current interest, e.g. the decimation of the Amazon rain forest
- school-based and community-based citizenship activities
- different forms of individual and group action, including decision-making and campaigning
- work with community partners and organisations on issues and problems in your community, e.g. developing better leisure and recreation facilities for young people
- considering the legal, moral, economic, environmental, historical and social aspects of different political problems and issues
- considering how a topic of interest is relevant to different contexts (school, neighbourhood, local, regional, national, European, international and global)
- using and interpreting different types of media and ICT
- making links between citizenship and work in other subjects.

Assessment consists of 40% examination and 60% controlled assessment.

Citizenship Studies at A level

The main elements of Citizenship at A level include:

- what it means to be British
- rights and responsibilities
- prejudice and discrimination
- democracy, active citizenship and participation
- crime, justice and punishment
- politics, power and participation
- global issues and making a difference.

Citizenship Studies and choosing a career

If you are interested in Citizenship Studies, you may wish to look at careers in areas such as the civil service, journalism, the law, local government, the police, or youth or community work.

Further information

- Active Citizenship   www.continyou.org.uk/what_we_do/healthy_active_learning_communities/active_citizenship

- The Citizenship Project   www.thecitizenproject.co.uk

CLASSICAL CIVILISATION/STUDIES

Classical Civilisation is the term used for a particular period in cultural history, that is, Ancient Greece and the Roman Empire. The period begins around the 7th century BC and continues through to the fall of the Roman Empire in the 5th century AD.

The course looks at life in both civilisations and at the literature produced by writers from the two civilisations.

GCSE Classical Civilisation

To study Classical Civilisation, it isn't necessary that you should have studied this in Key Stage 3. However, some knowledge of languages, particularly of Latin or Greek, and/or classical culture is useful.

Main elements of the course

The outline below is based on what the majority of exam board syllabuses include. For an exact description of the syllabus you will be studying, you will need to contact your school or the exam board itself.

The topics studied will include some of the following:

- Greek religion
- home and family in Athens
- Greek athletic and theatrical festivals
- Greek art and architecture
- Sparta and the Spartan system
- Roman religion
- Roman home and family life
- Roman sport and leisure
- Pompeii
- Roman Britain
- Greek literature (Homer, Sophocles, Euripides, Aristophanes)
- Roman literature (Herodotus, Virgil, Ovid, Pliny, Tacitus, Catullus, Livy, and Plautus).

How is Classical Civilisation taught and assessed?

Much of the work is teacher-led but you will need to do quite a lot of learning by reading the textbooks, and searching the Internet and other materials.

In Classical Civilisation, instead of doing coursework that is set and marked by your teacher, you will do controlled assessments. The controlled assessment component accounts for 25% of the final marks. The remaining 75% is allocated to examination work.

Classical Civilisation at A level

The main elements of the A level course will include:

- Greek literature and theatre
- Greek art and architecture
- Roman literature
- Roman art and architecture.

Classical Civilisation and choosing a career

There are few jobs directly related to Classical Civilisation. However, this course will encourage you to develop critical and **evaluative skills**, which will be of help in a wide range of A level courses and in many areas of employment.

Jobs that might benefit from study in this area include archaeologist, historian, lawyer, librarian, languages teacher and media work.

Further information

- Ancient Greece   www.ancientgreece.com

- Ancient History   http://ancienthistory.about.com/

- Catalogue of Internet resources   http://bubl.ac.uk/link/g/greece.htm;
                                       http://bubl.ac.uk/link/g/greekhistory.htm;
                                       http://bubl.ac.uk/link/g/greekliterature.htm;
                                       http://bubl.ac.uk/link/r/romanhistory.htm;
                                       http://bubl.ac.uk/link/r/romanarchaeologyinbritain.htm

- The Classics Pages   www.classicspage.com

DESIGN AND TECHNOLOGY

Design and Technology is a creative and practical subject. You learn how products are designed, created and used. This includes both creative and artistic designing as well as design and technology in the industrial context. You will have the opportunity to use tools (including ICT) and materials when designing and making things.

GCSE Design and Technology

You will take part in designing and making projects that are linked to your own interests, and are used in industry and in the community. Your projects could be an enterprise activity, where you identify an opportunity, design a product to meet a need, manufacture the product and evaluate the whole design-and-make process. You will use ICT to help with your work, including computer-aided design CAD/CAM software, control programs and ICT-based sources for research. You will learn how technology affects society and your own life, and also learn about both the advantages and disadvantages of new technologies.

The main choices in GCSE Design and Technology are:

- electronics/electronic products
- food technology
- graphics/graphic products
- industrial design
- product design
- resistant materials
- textiles technology.

Short course in Design and Technology

There is also a short course GCSE in this subject (with similar options to those listed above). The main difference is that the short courses take half the time allocated to a full GCSE.

How is Design and Technology taught and assessed?

You will do a mixture of teacher-led activities and 'hands-on' practical work. You will learn much of the theory through the investigations you do and the challenges you tackle. You will have to prepare and submit a portfolio and/or ICT evidence and a product that demonstrates your knowledge of materials, components, processes and techniques. You will also learn how to evaluate your own and others' work and consider the wider effects of design and technology on society. Some group work is usually involved and there may be considerable use of ICT.

Assessment consists of 60% controlled assessment and 40% examination, for both the full and short courses.

Design and Technology (or Product Design) at A level

The main elements of Design and Technology at A level are:

- design and technology capability
- industrial and commercial products and practices
- materials, components and systems
- product development.

Some exam boards offer separate A levels in different aspects of Design and Technology such as Fashion and Textiles, Food Technology, Resistant Materials Technology, and Systems Control Technology.

Design and Technology and choosing a career

Design and Technology can be a useful subject for you if you wish to leave school at 16 to go down the Apprenticeship route. There are Apprenticeships in Construction, Manufacturing or Engineering. If you have good IT skills, there is the possibility of starting at technician level in computer-aided design or engineering.

At graduate level, related jobs include exhibition/display designer, fashion designer, information scientist, production engineer, production manager, quality assurance officer, technical sales engineer, and textile designer.

Further information

- BBC GCSE Bitesize   www.bbc.co.uk/schools/gcsebitesize/design; www.bbc.co.uk/schools/gcsebitesize/dida

- Catalogue of Internet resources   http://bubl.ac.uk/link/d/designeducation.htm; http://bubl.ac.uk/link/t/technologyeducation.htm

- D&T Online   www.dtonline.org

- Design Council   www.designcouncil.org.uk

- Design-Technology   www.design-technology.info/subsectionlinks/default.htm

- Edu Scan   www.eduscan.info/technology/index.html

- How Stuff Works   www.howstuffworks.com

DRAMA

Drama covers all the different things involved in putting on a performance, including backstage work such as lighting, costumes and make-up. It involves a lot of practical work, group work and learning how to analyse production techniques.

GCSE Drama

GCSE Drama (or Drama and the Theatre Arts) follows on from the drama work that you will have done at Key Stage 3 (or equivalent). GCSE Drama is an excellent choice for anyone who wants to work in the performing arts. A GCSE in Drama will give you the opportunity to develop particular creative and imaginative skills. It will also help you develop confidence in communicating with other people, leadership skills, the ability to work well in a team, and other skills that are essential in all sorts of work with other people.

Main elements of the course

The outline below is based on what the majority of exam board syllabuses include. For an exact description of the syllabus you will be studying, you will need to contact your school or the exam board itself.

The syllabuses offered by the exam boards vary considerably but all of them have a good mixture of theoretical and practical work. The main elements are:

- study of drama and theoretical approaches to the medium of drama
- study of drama texts and the way drama is used both to communicate the playwright's ideas and to portray characters
- practical experience of writing, producing or performing in a play.

You will look at many aspects of devising, producing and performing a play, including set design, costume, make-up, lighting, sound, stage management, as well as acting (including improvisation).

You can also expect to have some experience of seeing professional productions and learning how to critically analyse such live productions.

How is Drama taught and assessed?

Assessment consists of 60% controlled assessment and 40% examination.

The course is largely practical and much of the work is done in groups. You will have the opportunity to create your own work and to use drama to express your feelings and ideas about a range of issues. You will probably have the choice of being involved in the performance of a play from an existing script or one you could create yourselves.

On the theoretical side, you will study plays written by other people, looking at how playwrights express their ideas about a theme or topic. You will also explore ways in which a play can be made to work effectively on the stage.

The exam for GCSE Drama is a practical performance. It is worth 40% of the marks. You will take part in a play that you have created as a group or rehearsed from a script. You can either be examined on your acting skills in the performance or on your design and technical skills (stage design, costume, masks and make-up, lighting or sound). You will perform the play in front of an audience and the examiner will be present at one of the performances.

For the 60% controlled assessment part of the course you can expect to be assessed on your performance in:

- responding to ideas and issues
- developing and exploring ideas in creating a piece of drama work
- presenting your ideas to an audience
- evaluating your own performance and that of others.

Drama and Theatre Studies at A level

There are courses in Drama and Theatre Studies at AS and A2, and a BTEC National in Performing Arts. The syllabuses vary but include the study of texts and preparation for performance, including the full range of drama and theatre activity, including performance, directing, stage design and lighting.

Drama and choosing a career

For a career in performance or on the technical side, it's usually necessary to think in terms of further study. You could go on to take an AS or A level in Drama and Theatre Studies, an Applied A level in Performing Arts, or a BTEC National Certificate or Diploma in Performing Arts or Performance Design and Technology. Some people enter theatre work after A levels, aiming to work their way up from backstage or box office work, or through another junior role in administration.

The traditional route to becoming an actor or performer is through a degree course or other form of professional training. Other careers at graduate level that you could think of are arts administrator, community art worker, drama therapist, journalist, programme researcher, stage manager, television production assistant, theatre director and wardrobe manager.

There are many other jobs not directly related to theatre, where it is useful to have had experience of drama, or where you will need to use some of the skills that can be developed during a GCSE Drama course. These might include, for example, jobs in retail, travel and tourism, sales and marketing or any area of work that involves meeting and working with people.

Further information

- BBC GCSE Bitesize   www.bbc.co.uk/schools/gcsebitesize/drama

- National Association of Youth Theatres   www.nayt.org.uk

- National Council for Drama Training   www.ncdt.co.uk

- Sparknotes – Drama   www.sparknotes.com/drama/

ENGINEERING (APPLIED GCSE)

Engineering is likely to appeal to you if you are interested in doing and making things, have an inquisitive mind and enjoy solving problems. You will need to take easily to technical learning and enjoy the idea of working to a design brief and then presenting your solution for an audience or for assessment. Note that many girls go on to make excellent engineers and should not be put off by the wrong-headed idea that engineering is a career sector for boys only.

GCSE Engineering

Engineering can be taken as either a Single or Double Award GCSE. At either level, this is a work-related course that allows you to do more practical work. This is done alongside the science and technology theory covered in the classroom. The course helps you understand how products are made and to learn about engineering systems and services.

The Double Award syllabus is equivalent to two standard GCSEs and it takes 2 years to complete.

GCSE Engineering is a demanding technical course and you will need good predicted grades in Maths, English and Science if you are to make a success of it.

Main elements of the course

The outline below is based on what the majority of exam board syllabuses include. For an exact description of the syllabus you will be studying, you will need to contact your school or the exam board itself.

How is Engineering taught and assessed?

The Double Award GCSE is made up of four compulsory units: the two corresponding Single Award GCSE units and two more units. Two units are externally assessed and two units are internally assessed and externally moderated.

The Single Award GCSE can be taken as either a 'stand-alone' qualification or as the first half (and 50%) of the Double Award. The Single Award is made up of two compulsory units: one is externally assessed and the other is internally assessed and externally moderated. The Single Award units are assessed at the same standard as the Double Award.

For the design and graphical communication unit, you will need to develop a portfolio of work to demonstrate what you have learnt. This will include the design process, client design briefs, design specifications, solutions, scientific and technological principles, the use of engineering drawings, and the communication of design solutions. You will be expected to apply the knowledge that you've gained to design and communicate solutions to technical problems. Your portfolio will be internally assessed by your teacher(s).

The engineered products unit is about understanding the process of designing a product and then producing it. It tests your planning and design skills. Once you have created a technical design, you will have to decide how to manufacture it, select the right materials, and ensure you apply quality control measures. Assessment is again via a portfolio and teacher assessment.

In the application of technology unit, you evaluate the problem and assess the evidence provided from measurements that may be mechanical, electrical or statistical. For this unit, your judgements and conclusions will be tested through an externally set examination.

Throughout the course there is an emphasis on sustainability and reducing waste in the engineering system.

The unit assessments can either all be taken at the end of the course in a linear fashion, or be used as part of a modular approach to the syllabus. Your teachers will decide which approach is best for teaching and learning in your school or college. However, there are two national rules on the method of assessment: 40% of the assessment must happen (by examination) at the end of the course and only one re-sit of each assessment unit is allowed.

Applied Engineering at A level

The main elements of Applied Engineering at A level are:

- engineering materials, processes and techniques
- the role of the engineer
- principles of design, planning and prototyping
- applied engineering systems
- the engineering environment
- applied design, planning and prototyping.

Engineering and choosing a career

Engineering is a very broad and flexible course, whether you are taking the GCSE or a Youth Apprenticeship (or both). You can use it as a springboard to go on to university (via A level, a Diploma in Engineering or Manufacturing and Product Design or a BTEC National) or do an Apprenticeship to further develop your skills. There are Apprenticeships in engineering and construction available at 16+, although their availability is sometimes limited at local level, so you may need to move away.

If you wish to work at professional engineering level, you need to plan for continued study to degree level and beyond. The main categories of engineering work are: engineering research and development, engineering design, installation and commissioning engineering, process engineering and customer services, manufacturing and processing, rail engineering and information technology and management services.

Further information

- Catalogue of Internet Resources   http://bubl.ac.uk/link/e/engineeringeducation.htm

- Why Study Materials?   www.whystudymaterials.ac.uk

- Garner, Gesaldine, *Careers in Engineering*, McGraw-Hill

- *How to Get Ahead In … Engineering and Design*, Raintree

ENGLISH

English is a compulsory subject at Key Stage 4. This usually means taking GCSE English or GCSE English Language and GCSE English Literature as two separate qualifications. In some schools English and English Literature may be taught as a combined course, but still lead to the two qualifications. Entry level English is available for those who may find the GCSE too demanding at this stage.

English is the key subject for learning how to communicate with others in school and in the wider world. Good understanding and use of English is essential for all curriculum subjects. Studying English involves reading a variety of books, learning to write in different styles, expressing your ideas in both creative and formal ways, and listening and discussing.

GCSE English

GCSE English is about learning the essential communication skills in speaking, listening, reading and writing. You will learn to express yourself creatively and imaginatively, and to communicate with others confidently and effectively. Spelling, grammar and punctuation are an essential part of studying English.

Main elements of the course

The current specifications for GCSEs in English and English literature end in August 2011. New GCSE specifications in these subjects were accredited in autumn 2009 for centres to plan for first teaching from September 2010.

The main topics will certainly continue to include:

- use of English in the daily world, including media texts
- original writing
- studying written language texts
- speaking and listening
- writing to argue/persuade/advise
- writing to explain/inform/describe.

The range of reading varies across England, Wales and Northern Ireland, but in all three countries this must include prose, poetry and drama. There will also usually be some study of texts from different cultures and traditions.

Variations

You might be offered a Certificate in English as an alternative to (or alongside) GCSE English. The Certificate is for people who can use everyday written and spoken English to a good level, but who might struggle to achieve a GCSE in the subject at this stage.

How is English taught and assessed?

There will be lots of teacher-led activity, but you can also expect to participate in a variety of speaking and listening assessments through the course. These contribute to 20% of the final English grade. You will do a variety of reading, including drama, poetry, fiction, non-fiction and media texts. You will also produce a range of written work. Controlled assessment assignments can last for several weeks, with part of the work done in class and part at home. Other assessment may include extended individual contributions, group discussion and interaction, and drama-focused activities.

Assessment consists of 60% controlled assessment and 40% examination. For English Literature, the weighting is 30% controlled assessment and 70% examination.

GCSE English and Functional Skills

In the same way that Level 1 Functional Skills in English are part of the Key Stage 3 programme of study for English, the Key Stage 4 programme of study reflects the functional English standards at Level 2. The skills that you will learn centre around the basic functions of speaking, listening, reading and writing. The aim is that you should be confident and capable of using these skills and should be able to communicate effectively by adapting to your audience and the context of the communication. This includes being able to explain information clearly and succinctly in speech and writing, expressing a point of view reasonably and persuasively, and using ICT to communicate effectively.

In life and work each individual should be able to:

- read and understand information and instructions
- use this understanding to act appropriately
- analyse how ideas and information are presented
- evaluate the usefulness of ideas and information, for example in solving a problem
- make an oral presentation or report
- contribute to discussions and use speech to work collaboratively in teams to agree actions and conclusions.

Your school or college should provide you relevant opportunities and contexts for testing of these functional elements of GCSE English. Schools and colleges are due to introduce the revised GCSE in English, including Functional Skills, in September 2009.

English/English Language at A level

The main elements include:

- interacting through language
- introduction to language study
- language variation and change
- using language.

The exam boards also offer a combined course in English Language and Literature.

English and choosing a career

As with the other core subjects (Mathematics and ICT), the relevance of English as a subject is far greater in its general application to just about all vocational pathways than it is in any one single pathway. Employers want people who can communicate effectively in both the written and spoken word – and the need is at least as great if you are self-employed. In this sense, English is very much a vocational subject. Again as with the other core subjects, for most of us it supports other job-specific skills: for example, the engineer or architect who wants to progress will need to show good ability in English and communication skills.

If you do wish to use your English language and communication skills as a main feature of your future working life, you could consider jobs in, for example, administration, customer service, information science, journalism, marketing and sales, and public relations.

Among the graduate-level areas of employment for the English specialist are the areas of advertising, journalism, marketing, public relations, publishing, teaching (including teaching English as a foreign or second language), and television and film work.

Further information

* BBC GCSE Bitesize   www.bbc.co.uk/schools/gcsebitesize/english
* BBC Skillswise   www.bbc.co.uk/skillswise
* Catalogue of Internet resources   http://bubl.ac.uk/link/e/englishlanguageeducation.htm
* English GCSE Guide   www.gcseguide.co.uk/englishgcseguide.htm

ENGLISH LITERATURE

While studying Literature you learn about the experiences of people from different countries and different periods of history. This contributes to our sense of cultural identity. The study of English Literature involves the reading of stories, poetry and drama, as well as non-fiction and media texts.

GCSE English Literature

The accreditation end date of the current GCSE in English Literature is August 2011. A new GCSE specification was accredited in autumn 2009 for first teaching from September 2010. Assessments will not be available until late 2010 at the earliest.

GCSE English Literature involves the study and analysis of texts such as novels, poetry and plays, including contemporary writing. You will also understand how writers use language to achieve different effects and will learn about historical and social influences on writing.

Main elements of the course

The outline below is based on what the majority of exam board syllabuses include. For an exact description of the syllabus you will be studying, you will need to contact your school or the exam board itself.

GCSE English Literature requires study of several different texts, including prose, poetry and drama, both pre- and post-1914.

How is English Literature taught and assessed?

You will need do a lot of independent reading in the study of literature. Classwork involves studying parts of the set texts in detail, but supporting reading will be necessary outside the classroom. English Literature is a demanding subject in terms of both the amount of reading and the number of essays you will need to write. You also may be encouraged to enact a section of the play you are studying. Group visits to a theatre are sometimes arranged, and you will also be encouraged to make your own individual visits where this is possible and appropriate. It is, of course, particularly beneficial to be able to see a professional production of any play you are actually studying.

In English Literature, instead of doing coursework that is set and marked by your teacher, you will do controlled assessments.

English Literature at A level

English Literature at A level involves the study of set texts, from drama, poetry and fiction. A Shakespeare play is often one of the set texts.

The choice of poetry may include some of Chaucer's *Canterbury Tales* and/or Shakespeare's sonnets. Other poets that may be studied are William Blake, Robert Browning, T. S. Eliot, Seamus Heaney, John Keats, John Milton, Sylvia Plath, Percy Bysshe Shelley, Alfred Lord Tennyson, William Wordsworth.

The choice of texts can include books by pre-20th-century writers of fiction such as: Jane Austen, Charlotte Brontë, Emily Brontë, Joseph Conrad, Daniel Defoe, Charles Dickens, Henry Fielding, Elizabeth Gaskell, Thomas Hardy, Henry James, Robert Louis Stevenson, Anthony Trollope and H. G. Wells.

The exam boards also offer a combined course in English Language and Literature.

English Literature and choosing a career

Usually this subject is best regarded as an interesting subject in its own right, rather than one that will link directly with a particular career. However, as with English Language, it is an excellent subject for improving how you communicate in your everyday language. The analytical and critical skills that it helps develop are also of great help in many jobs.

If you particularly enjoy the study of literature, there are some jobs that are more directly related to this area of study. These include library assistant, marketing, tour guide, and many other jobs that require good communication skills.

At graduate level, jobs for the lover of English literature include advertising, arts administration, journalism, marketing, public relations, publishing, and television and film work.

Further information

- BBC GCSE Bitesize   www.bbc.co.uk/schools/gcsebitesize/english
- Catalogue of Internet Resources   http://bubl.ac.uk/link/e/engishdrama.htm; http://bubl.ac.uk/link/e/englishliterature.htm
- National Council for the Training of Journalists   www.nctj.com
- Sparknotes – Literature   www.sparknotes.com/lit/
- Sparknotes – Poetry   www.sparknotes.com/poetry/
- Sparknotes – Shakespeare   www.sparknotes.com/Shakespeare/

GEOGRAPHY

Geography teaches you about the changing world in which we live, in terms of both the physical and the human environment.

GCSE Geography

Geography consists of physical and human geography – you learn about the environment in which we live and the way that humans interact with and manage that environment.

Main elements of the course

The outline below is based on what the majority of exam board syllabuses include. For an exact description of the syllabus you will be studying, you will need to contact your school or the exam board itself.

There are three main areas of study in Geography – physical, environmental and human geography. In physical geography you study the natural features such as weather and climate, rivers and coastal landscapes. Human geography covers population and economic and industrial activity, including agriculture, tourism and the manufacturing industries. Environmental geography looks at how the natural environment shapes our lives and how human action impacts on the environment, including the use of energy, the management of ecosystems, and the management of change and development. Overlapping areas include the relationship between people and their environments, and sustainable development. You will learn to use maps, statistics and photographs and take part in field trips and other out-of-classroom learning.

Short course

The short course GCSE requires half of the study of the full course and can be completed in half of the time allocated to the full GCSE over 2 years or in 1 year with the same timetable commitment as a full GCSE. The content is part of the content of the full course, with syllabuses maintaining a balanced approach to the subject.

How is Geography taught and assessed?

Much of the work is teacher-led but you will need to do some learning from textbooks and other materials. However, the subject does involve more practical work – for example, with maps, statistical data, weather reports and case study material. You will carry out surveys, create questionnaires and watch film or video. The analysis of data and the use of technology are important aspects of Geography at all levels.

In Geography, instead of doing coursework that is teacher-set and marked you will do controlled assessments. The controlled assessment component accounts for 25% of the final marks. The controlled assessment is usually based on a single fieldwork-based investigation. The remaining 75% is allocated to examination work.

Geography at A level

The main elements of A level Geography are:

- challenge and change in the natural environment
- core concepts in human geography
- core concepts in physical geography.

Geography and choosing a career

Relatively few people make active use of geography in their career. However, the subject encourages the development of a wide range of skills – in research, numeracy and spatial awareness, and in critical and analytical thinking. All of these can be of great value when starting on a range of careers, no matter what age you are.

If you are interested in a job more closely related to geography itself, it is usually necessary to study the subject (or a related one) to degree level first. Examples of jobs which do use the skills and knowledge of the geographer include: cartographer, distribution/logistics manager, ecologist, environment consultant, geologist, mining engineer, surveyor, town planner, and transportation planner.

Further information

- Association for Geographic Information   www.agi.org.uk

- BBC GCSE Bitesize   www.bbc.co.uk/schools/gcsebitesize/geography

- BBC Science and Nature: Earth   www.bbc.co.uk/science/space/solarsystem/earth

- Catalogue of Internet Resources   http://bubl.ac.uk/link/g/geographyeducation.htm

- Internet Geography   www.geography.learnontheinternet.co.uk

- National Geographic   www.nationalgeographic.com

- Royal Geographical Society   www.rgs.org

- UK Civil Service Careers   www.civilservice.gov.uk/jobs

HEALTH AND SOCIAL CARE (APPLIED GCSE)

In Health and Social Care you will learn about health services, the care industry, the promotion of health and well-being, the nature of personal relationships and the various stages of personal development. You don't need to have studied health or social care before starting the GCSE. It is important that you have a lively and enquiring mind, an interest in the subject area and an ability to communicate your ideas effectively.

GCSE Health and Social Care

There are Single Award and Double Award options. You study two units for the Single Award and an additional two units for the Double Award. The units provide a broad introduction to a wide range of health and social care issues.

The GCSE in Health and Social Care will provide you with the technical knowledge, skills and understanding that you will need in a health or social care workplace or in further education or training. There will be an opportunity for work-related learning to help you to decide if this is the right area of work for you.

The Single Award is both a 'stand-alone' qualification and also the first half of the GCSE Double Award. It is made up of two compulsory units:

- health, social care and early years provision
- understanding personal development and relationships.

The Double Award is made up these same two units, plus two more compulsory units:

- promoting health and well-being
- safeguarding and protecting individuals.

How is Health and Social Care taught and assessed?

This is an Applied GCSE and its teaching is therefore closely related to the health and care work sector. The subject is taught through a mixture of teacher-led activities and independent assignments, research and reading. Much of the learning is of a practical nature. There are likely to be visiting speakers who will talk about their work and/or current issues in the health and social care sector. You may also make group visits to different health and social care settings.

Assessment consists of 60% controlled assessment and 40% examination.

Health and Social Care A level

The Applied A level course usually includes a mixture of compulsory units and some optional ones from a range of choices. The core modules include areas such as:

- communication in health and social care
- equal opportunities and clients' rights

- factors affecting human growth and development
- physical aspects of health
- research perspectives in health and social care
- social care and early years services.

Other units fall into three broad categories:

- biological, psychological and medical factors relating to health and social care
- health and social care relating to people in their early years
- health care provision and policy.

Health and Social Care and choosing a career

Many students who invest additional time in taking this applied course will already be actively considering working in the broad occupational area. Specific jobs include: care assistant, childminder, dental hygienist, health promotion/education specialist, health care assistant, mental health nurse, midwife, nurse, nursery nurse, play worker, pre-school/nursery school assistant, social worker.

For higher-level occupations in health and social care, you will certainly need to continue your studies through A levels, a relevant Diploma, NVQ or Apprenticeship – and possibly beyond. If you wish to become a doctor, for example, the preferred route remains taking three sciences at A level (or two science A levels plus A level Mathematics). Increasingly, senior jobs in other branches of medicine, health and social care also require graduate entry. Examples include health promotion, health service management, lifestyle coaching and consultancy, medical sales, nursing, nutrition, occupational therapy, pharmacy, physiotherapy, teaching, and working with people with disabilities.

The Diploma in Social Work (**DipSW**) is currently the professional qualification for all social workers and education welfare officers in England. The DipSW course is offered at several levels at universities and colleges of higher education throughout England. The course takes a minimum of 2 years to complete.

Further information

- Catalogue of Internet resources	http://bubl.ac.uk/link/h/healthcare.htm
- Jobs in community care	www.communitycare.co.uk
- **NHS** Careers	www.nhscareers.nhs.uk
- Sparknotes – Health	www.sparknotes.com/health/
- *Careers in Health Care*, McGraw-Hill
- *How to Get Ahead in … Healthcare*, Raintree
- Alexander, Laurel, *Nursing and Midwifery Uncovered*, Trotman
- Caprez, Emma, *Real Life Guide to Care*, Trotman
- *Working in Community Healthcare*, VT Lifeskills
- *Working in Hospitals*, VT Lifeskills

HISTORY

History is about knowledge and understanding of the past, of your local area, your country and the world as a whole. However, history is not just learning about the past. Through developing your view of the past from the perspective of the present, you can interpret and understand current events.

GCSE History

The study of GCSE History helps you gain knowledge and understanding of various aspects of the past at a local, national and international levels. The subject also helps you develop many useful skills and qualities, including empathy, the critical evaluation of written information and the ability to weigh up evidence.

The common elements of all GCSE History courses include:

- knowledge and understanding of the past
- interpretation of historical events and activities
- developing the skills of historical enquiry
- developing organisational and communication skills.

In addition, there has to be a minimum of 25% subject content that relates to British history and/or the history of England, Scotland, Ireland or Wales.

There are two main courses:

- modern world history
- Schools History Project.

Main elements of course

The Schools History Project topics include:

- medicine through time or media through time
- the American West 1840–1895
- Britain 1815–1951
- Elizabethan England 1558–1603
- Germany 1919–1945.

The modern world history topics will usually include:

- British history
- international relations in the 20th century
- a specific period of foreign history (e.g. in Germany, Russia or USA).

Short course

There is a short course GCSE available in History (as well as another one in Ancient History). The main difference is that the course takes half the time allocated to a full GCSE.

See also the introduction to short courses on page 8.

How is History taught and assessed?

As well as teacher-led activity and group discussion, you will learn to investigate a range of resources, including books, newspapers, artefacts, historical sites and the Internet to explore the past. You need to be aware that, in choosing this subject, you will be committing yourself to do a considerable amount of reading and writing.

In History, instead of doing coursework that is set and marked by your teacher, you will do controlled assessments. Assessment consists of 25% controlled assessment and 75% examination.

History at A level

The main variation in the A level History syllabus is the type of history studied (social, political or religious history) and a possible focus on a particular period. Most syllabuses include the study of a particular period of English or British history: the courses tend to select a period of up to 150 years at a time. You may also study a period of history other than British or English history. The same applies in terms of the length of period studied, but in general the periods offered for study for European or world history run from about 1,000 to 1,900 years and not more recent than that.

Most courses will cover:

- a range of historical perspectives
- a substantial element of English history
- continuity and change over a particular period
- significant historical events, issues or people
- the diversity of society
- the history of more than one country or state.

Some syllabuses include the opportunity to study certain historical themes, for example:

- Civil Rights in the USA 1865–1980
- rebellion and disorder in England 1485–1603
- the Catholic Reformation in the 16th century
- the decline of Spain 1598–1700
- war and society in Britain 1793–1918.

History and choosing a career

Relatively few students go on to make active use of their history studies in their working lives. However, the skills and knowledge gained are very useful in a wide range of occupations, including law, management and administration, sales and marketing.

There are many jobs that do draw specifically on the skills and techniques of the historian. These include: archaeologist, archivist, costume designer, genealogist, librarian, media researcher, museum work and tourist guide.

Further information

- BBC GCSE Bitesize   www.bbc.co.uk/schools/gcsebitesize/history

- BBC History   www.bbc.co.uk/history

- Catalogue of Internet Resources   http://bubl.ac.uk/link/h/historyeducation.htm

- Council for British Archaeology   www.britarch.ac.uk

- The History Channel   www.history.co.uk

- History Learning Site   www.historylearningsite.co.uk

- Museums Association   www.museumsassociation.org

- School History   www.schoolhistory.co.uk

- Sparknotes – History   www.sparknotes.com/history/

INFORMATION AND COMMUNICATION TECHNOLOGY (ICT)

ICT is about the purpose and use of communication systems, including how ICT is used to solve problems. You can expect to learn about hardware and software, the effect of new technology on the world and how to present work using ICT.

ICT is a compulsory National Curriculum subject. For most students this will mean taking a GCSE or Applied GCSE in ICT, a qualification from the DiDA suite of awards (see below), or perhaps Entry level ICT.

GCSE ICT

Computers and information technology have clearly come to play an important part in all our everyday lives. Even if we choose not be actively involved in the technology, that is, we just use it rather than produce it, it is all around us, every day of our lives. As a subject, ICT involves the study of how information and communications systems can be used and how they can solve problems. You will learn about hardware and software, the effect of new technology on the world and how to present your work using ICT.

Main elements of the course

The current specification for GCSE in ICT ends in August 2011. The new GCSE specification in this subject was accredited in autumn 2009 for centres to plan for first teaching from September 2010.

The outline below is based on what the majority of exam board syllabuses include. For an exact description of the syllabus you will be studying, you will need to contact your school or the exam board itself.

Topics in GCSE ICT include:

- data communications
- databases
- hardware
- ICT systems
- implications of ICT
- measurement and control
- modelling
- software
- the legal framework.

Applied ICT

Applied ICT is a vocational course that should appeal to you if you like using computers and want to know more about ICT systems, and how organisations use ICT, ICT tools, spreadsheets, word processing, presentation techniques and multimedia software.

DiDA (Diploma in Digital Applications)

DiDA is actually a suite of three qualifications: the Award (AiDA), the Certificate (CiDA) and the Diploma (DiDA). So if you opt for this type of ICT qualification, you will be able to progress through the suite, if you wish to.

- The Award is the equivalent of one GCSE.
- The Certificate is to the value of two GCSEs.
- The Diploma is the equivalent of four GCSEs.

These are entirely paperless qualifications that will help you learn practical and transferable ICT skills. You will learn to apply your knowledge and skills to real-life situations. Therefore, you will present the evidence of your work in an 'e-portfolio', which will be assessed and moderated on-screen (on the computer).

Current DiDA topics include:

- graphics
- games authoring
- ICT in enterprise
- multimedia
- using ICT.

How is ICT taught and assessed?

ICT involves studying what information and communication systems can be used for and how they can solve certain problems. You learn about hardware and software, the effect of new technology on the world and how to present work using ICT.

In ICT, you will learn to:

- use technology well to organise yourself, your work and your learning
- apply ICT to real-world situations when solving problems and carrying out a range of tasks and enquiries
- think about how you can find out more about and use more advanced or new ICT tools and information sources
- evaluate your experiences of using ICT
- use ICT in other subjects and areas of learning.

In GCSE ICT assessment is 40–60% controlled assessment plus a written examination for the rest of the marks. For the Applied ICT this changes to two-thirds controlled assessment and one-third written test.

GCSE ICT and Functional Skills

In the same way that Level 1 Functional Skills in ICT are a part of the Key Stage 3 programme of study for ICT, the Key Stage 4 programme of study reflects the Functional ICT Skills at Level 2. The aim is that each individual should be confident and capable when using ICT systems and tools to meet a variety of needs in a range of contexts. For example, you will use ICT to find, select and bring together relevant information and use ICT to develop, interpret and exchange information, for a purpose.

Applied ICT at A level

The main elements of an ICT A level are:

- information, systems and communications
- structured practical ICT tasks
- practical applications of ICT using standard/generic applications software
- communications technology and its application
- ICT project
- ICT systems and systems management.

ICT and choosing a career

Whether or not you choose to be an ICT specialist, in most jobs it will be an advantage to have had a good grounding in ICT and to have some knowledge of how computers and information technology can be put to best use. A good grasp of this field will open up opportunities whether you opt to leave school at 16 or carry on with further studies prior to entry into the world of work. The vast majority of organisations rely on IT support in some shape or form.

The higher level specialist jobs may require degree qualifications, although there are also prestigious non-graduate qualifications valued within the industry. Examples of graduate or graduate-level jobs for the IT specialist include: applications developer, artificial intelligence researcher, computer games designer, computer service technician, database administrator, Internet/web professional, IT consultant, IT sales professional, multimedia designer, penetration testing consultant, robotics developer, software developer/engineer/ programmer, systems analyst/designer/developer, and technical support person.

Further information

- BBC GCSE Bitesize   www.bbc.co.uk/schools/gcsebitesize/ict
- BBC Webwise   www.bbc.co.uk/webwise
- British Computer Society   www.bcs.org
- Computer Information Center www.compinfo-center.com
- ICT Teacher   www.ict-teacher.com
- IT Careers   www.computeach.co.uk/Jegsworks
                             www.jegsworks.com/Lessons/
                             lessonintro.htm

- Hobbs, Mike, *E-Commerce Uncovered*, Trotman
- *How to Get Ahead In … IT and Administration*, Raintree

LEISURE AND TOURISM (APPLIED GCSE)

The study of Leisure and Tourism relates to a very large and varied work sector. At Key Stage 4, the emphasis will be principally on leisure, tourism and travel, but there are clear links to other areas, such as hospitality and sport.

GCSE Leisure and Tourism

There are Single and Double Award GCSEs in Leisure and Tourism. The Double Award is worth two GCSEs, while the Single Award is worth one GCSE. Both qualifications cover different areas of the leisure, tourism and travel industries, such as holiday resorts, theme parks, travel agencies and air transport. You will learn about customer service, marketing and tackling real workplace situations.

Main elements of the course

For the Double Award course, there are four compulsory units that cover the following aspects:

- understanding the wide extent of the leisure and tourism industry (entertainment, visitor attractions, cultural and leisure facilities, accommodation and travel)
- sales and promotion
- customer needs and services
- employment in the sector.

For the Single Award course, you take two units – one compulsory unit and one from a limited choice. The essential topics are the same as some of those studied in the Double Award:

- understanding the leisure and tourism industry
- customer needs and services.

For an exact description of the syllabus you will be studying, you will need to contact your school or the exam board itself.

How is Leisure and Tourism taught and assessed?

There will be a mixture of teacher-led activity, other classroom work, projects, investigations and other practical work. There will almost certainly be visits to different locations and organisations that are relevant to the study of this sector.

Assessment consists of 60% controlled assessment and 40% examination.

Applied Leisure and Recreation at A level

The main elements of an Applied Leisure and Recreation A level are:

- business systems in the leisure and recreation industry
- children's play
- countryside recreation
- customer service in leisure and recreation
- financial planning in leisure and recreation
- health and fitness
- human resources in leisure and recreation
- investigating anatomy and physiology
- investigating leisure and recreation
- marketing leisure and recreation
- outdoor activities
- providing coaching sessions
- safe working practices in the leisure and recreation industry
- sponsorship in sport
- sports officiating
- sports tourism
- the sports industry.

Leisure and Tourism and choosing a career

If you choose the Leisure and Tourism Applied course you are probably seriously considering taking up a career in the broad occupational area. On completion of the course, you can choose to further study the subject at A level or to do a BTEC National qualification in Travel and Tourism. Alternatively, you can move directly into work-based training. Trainee positions are quite commonly available, especially for those with A levels, for example with travel agencies and companies. Other specific jobs include: air cabin crew, customer services, holiday representative, hotel receptionist/front desk staff, and passenger check-in operator. Graduate jobs include holiday representative, tourism officer, tourist information centre manager, tour manager, and travel agency manager.

Further information

- Careers in Leisure and Learning   www.skillsactive.com/careers

- Institute of Travel and Tourism   www.itt.co.uk

- Travel Industry Jobs   www.travelindustryjobs.co.uk

- *How to Get Ahead In … Leisure and Tourism*, Raintree

- Evans, Sara, *Travel Industry Uncovered*, Trotman

MANUFACTURING (APPLIED GCSE)

The manufacturing sector is made up many different industries and includes, for example, the manufacture of food, drink, textiles, print, biological and chemical goods.

GCSE Manufacturing

A GCSE in Manufacturing will appeal to you if you want to learn about manufacturing and wish to progress to further/higher education or employment in the sector. You will gain an understanding of the contribution that manufacturing makes to society and the economy. You will need have a good standard of numeracy and literacy, as well as an interest in designing and making products.

GCSE Manufacturing can be taken as a Double or Single Award GCSE. Both qualifications look at how products are designed and made, and the importance of materials. You will learn how to develop a design specification, draw up a final design, and offer a manufacturing solution.

Main elements of the course

The outline below is based on what the majority of exam board syllabuses include. For an exact description of the syllabus you will be studying, you will need to contact your school or the exam board itself.

The basic topics for both Awards are:

- production details and constraints
- materials, components and/or ingredients and their constraints
- new technology used in and by the manufacturing industries
- impact of modern technologies
- manufactured products
- a range of manufacturing industries
- how to design a product
- how to manufacture a product.

For the Single Award, you have to complete two compulsory units, which are about the manufacture of a product and manufacturing processes. For the Double Award you must complete four compulsory units, covering the same areas as the Single Award, but with additional study of the manufacturing sector and the impact of modern technologies on manufacturing.

For both qualifications, you are required to design and manufacture a product yourself.

How is Manufacturing taught and assessed?

Teaching consists of teacher-led and other usual classroom activity, along with plenty of practical work. You will learn how to plan and carry out investigations and tasks, using a range of tools, equipment, materials, components and processes. You will be taught how to analyse issues and problems relevant to manufacturing processes and procedures. You will gather, record and analyse information, data and other forms of evidence. You will learn how to evaluate evidence, make judgements, and present conclusions accurately and appropriately.

Assessment consists of 60% controlled assessment and 40% examination.

Manufacturing and choosing a career

Many students who invest the additional time in taking the Manufacturing applied course will already be actively considering taking up a career in this area. Opportunities in manufacturing and engineering fall into the following broad categories:

- engineering research and development
- engineering design
- installation and commissioning engineering
- process engineering, control and maintenance
- commercial engineering and customer services
- manufacturing and processing
- information technology and management services.

Specific jobs include: electronics assembler, engineering operative, materials technician, product designer, production manager and quality control inspector.

Further information

- Institute of Operations Management   www.iomnet.org.uk

- SEMTA   www.semta.org.uk

MATHEMATICS

Mathematics is a compulsory National Curriculum subject at Key Stage 4. This usually means taking a GCSE in Mathematics, but if you find the GCSE too difficult at this stage you can do Entry level Mathematics. Mathematics involves learning about numbers, algebra, shapes, measurements and how to handle information. You also learn how to use your knowledge to solve real-life problems.

GCSE Mathematics

Since Mathematics is a compulsory subject, it is best to take the GCSE if you are capable of doing so. Mathematics is a subject that is useful in almost anything. It's also a specific requirement for a vast number of options in both employment and further/higher education.

A new GCSE specification is being tested for first teaching from September 2010. The new qualifications are intended to:

- improve attitudes towards Mathematics
- inspire young people to continue Mathematics studies beyond the age of 16
- meet the requirements of the revised secondary curriculum, including the introduction of functional skills.

Single GCSE in Mathematics

If you are starting your Key Stage 4 in 2010, you will most likely be taking the new single GCSE in Mathematics. The single GCSE in Mathematics introduced in 2010 reflects the programme of study for Key Stage 4.

For an exact description of the syllabus you will be studying, you will need to contact your school or the exam board itself.

Certain topics are common to GCSE Mathematics, at whatever tier it is studied. (See below for what is meant by 'tier'.) These topics include:

- practical applications of mathematics
- number and algebra
- shape, space and measures
- data handling and statistics.

The degree of detail to which you study each of these topics depends on the tier for which you are entered (see below for an explanation of tiering).

Linked pair GCSEs in Mathematics

As well as the new single GCSE in Mathematics, an alternative way to study mathematics – the linked pair of GCSE Mathematics qualifications – is being tested. Both the linked pair GCSEs and the single GCSE will cover the core National Curriculum programme of study. But the linked pair GCSE will give a broader grounding in both GCSEs: Methods in Mathematics and Applications of Mathematics. The Applications of Mathematics GCSE will focus mostly on showing you how mathematics works in the real world. Methods in Mathematics will focus on mathematical reasoning and analysis.

This second way is still being tested, so isn't widely available. Candidates for the 3-year pilot (test) programme will be drawn from several schools (and colleges) to include a range of learners, including those on Diploma programmes. The national roll out of the new programme is unlikely to start before September 2015.

Both the single GCSE and the new pilot qualifications will enable you to progress to Level 3 qualifications in Mathematics as well as other subjects.

How is Mathematics taught and assessed?

In Mathematics you can expect to:

- use a range of mathematical methods and techniques
- work on sequences of tasks that involve using the same mathematical principles in increasingly difficult or unfamiliar contexts, or increasingly demanding mathematics in similar contexts
- work on 'open' and 'closed' tasks in a variety of real and abstract contexts
- work on problems that arise in other subjects and in contexts beyond the school
- work on tasks that bring together different concepts, processes and mathematical content
- become familiar with a range of resources, including ICT.

The two-tier model for Mathematics is the same as that used in all other tiered subjects, e.g. English and Science. It has a higher tier covering grades A*–D and a foundation tier covering grades C–G. This allows all students to achieve a grade C, if their work deserves it.

GCSE Mathematics no longer includes coursework controlled assessment. All marks are awarded on the basis of the written examination(s).

If you are taking part in the linked pair pilot, you will be entered for both qualifications (and you will receive two separate grades).

GCSE Mathematics and Functional Skills

In the same way that Level 1 Functional Skills in Mathematics are a fundamental part of the Key Stage 3 programme of study for Mathematics, the Key Stage 4 programme of study reflects the functional Mathematics standards at Level 2. The aim is that each individual should have sufficient understanding of a range of mathematical concepts and should know how and when to use them. For example, you should have the confidence and capability to use mathematics to solve problems and to use a range of tools, including ICT, as appropriate.

In life and work, each individual should be able to:

- develop the analytical and reasoning skills to draw conclusions
- justify how these conclusions are reached

- identify errors or inconsistencies
- validate and interpret results
- judge the limits of the validity of these results
- use these results effectively and efficiently.

You should be given opportunities to test these functional elements of GCSE Mathematics, and schools and colleges are due to introduce the revised GCSE in Mathematics, including functional skills, in September 2010.

Mathematics at A level

A level Mathematics is divided into Pure Mathematics (theoretical mathematics) and Applied Mathematics (the application of the subject to different contexts and uses). The exam boards tend to give schools and colleges some choice about the options you can choose to study in the different mathematical areas. The main areas of study are:

- discrete mathematics
- mechanics
- pure mathematics
- statistics and probability.

This subject is also available at **AEA** level.

Mathematics and choosing a career

Although you would not become a professional mathematician on leaving school with GCSEs or even A levels, there are many employers looking for all-round numeracy and/or a particular strength in mathematics. Banking, building society work, insurance, payroll work and retail are examples of such areas of employment where junior positions are available after A levels, if not before.

Graduate jobs related to Mathematics include: accountancy, actuarial work, banking, economic and statistical work, financial advice and planning, insurance and pensions, management consultancy, quantity surveying, and scientific research and development.

Further information

- BBC GCSE Bitesize   www.bbc.co.uk/schools/gcsebitesize/maths
- BBC Skillswise   www.bbc.co.uk/skillswise
- Catalogue of Internet resources   http://bubl.ac.uk/link/m/mathematicseducation.htm
- Figure it out   www.bbc.co.uk/worldservice/sci_tech/features/figure_it_out
- Institute of Mathematics and its Applications   www.ima.org.uk
- Mathematics Careers   www.mathscareers.org.uk
- Mathematics GCSE Guide   www.gcseguide.co.uk/mathsgcseguide.htm
- Royal Statistical Society   www.rss.org.uk
- Sparknotes – Maths   www.sparknotes.com/math/

MODERN FOREIGN LANGUAGES

Although foreign languages are no longer compulsory at Key Stage 4, the government thinks that the learning of languages is highly desirable for all young people. It views languages as being crucially important in our modern knowledge society, and it's committed to improving the teaching and learning of languages in schools. The approach includes the introduction of an entitlement to languages for all pupils in Key Stage 2 (by 2009/10). Despite the removal of modern foreign languages from the statutory Key Stage 4 curriculum, it is hoped that there will be, over time, an increase in the number of people studying languages beyond school.

GCSEs in modern foreign languages

If you have shown evidence of some ability in language learning, you should certainly give serious consideration to carrying on with it – or even, more rarely, starting a new language for GCSE study. A GCSE in a modern foreign language is highly regarded by university admissions tutors, and employers also consider linguistic ability as a good skill to have in people they consider employing. If you have shown a particular talent for language learning, you should consider the option of taking two foreign languages, if your school will allow it: this may put you at an advantage should you later decide to apply for a degree course in languages.

The modern languages most commonly offered at GCSE by schools and colleges are French, German, Spanish and Italian. In addition, Gujarati, Polish, Punjabi, Russian and Urdu are all increasing in importance, and other languages may be taught in some schools. Welsh is an important element of the curriculum in Wales for those young people for whom Welsh is not their native tongue.

Main elements of the course

For an exact description of the syllabus you will be studying, you will need to contact your school or the exam board itself. Most language courses build on the work covered at Key Stage 3. The emphasis is on the four languages skills of:

- listening
- reading
- speaking
- writing.

Short course

Short course GCSEs are available in Dutch, French, German, Gujarati, Persian, Portuguese, Spanish and Turkish. The main difference is that the course takes half the time allocated to a full GCSE.

See also the introduction to short courses on page 8.

How are modern foreign languages taught and assessed?

Teaching is via a combination of teacher-led and interactive classroom activity, conversation work, written exercises, listening to the language and reading practice. Great importance is placed on communication, especially speaking.

In modern foreign languages, instead of doing coursework that is set and marked by your teacher, you will do controlled assessments, which now account for 60% of the marks. These include tests in listening, reading and speaking. The rest of the assessment is by examination; 10% of the total marks are allocated to knowledge and accurate application of grammar and structures. The use of dictionaries is no longer permitted.

The examination may be at one of two levels – Foundation and Higher. Your entry level will usually be decided quite late in the course.

Modern foreign languages at A level

Most of the modern foreign languages offered at GCSE can also be studied at A level. These include Chinese, Dutch, French, Gujarati, German, Italian, Portuguese, Russian, Spanish, and Urdu.

Study of a modern foreign language at A level will include:

- aspects of culture and society
- listening
- reading
- speaking
- writing.

Modern foreign languages and choosing a career

Being able to speak another language can be helpful in a wide range of careers. Language fluency is often a very useful skill in support of a job or career that is not specifically focused on languages, e.g. in engineering, media work, publishing, sales or science. Some jobs and careers will require more frequent use of linguistic skills. Examples include: courier, holiday representative, hotel receptionist, importer/exporter, interpreter, patent agent, police work, translator, work in the Diplomatic Service, and any job involving work abroad.

Further information

- BBC GCSE Bitesize
  www.bbc.co.uk/schools/gcsebitesize/french;
  www.bbc.co.uk/schools/gcsebitesize/german;
  www.bbc.co.uk/schools/gcsebitesize/spanish

- BBC Languages
  www.bbc.co.uk/languages

- Centre for Information on
  Language Teaching and Research
  www.cilt.org.uk

- français interactif
  www.laits.utexas.edu/fi/index.html

- Institute of Linguists and Interpreting
  www.iol.org.uk

- Institute of Translation and Interpreting
  www.iti.org.uk

- Learn Spanish: a free online tutorial
  www.studyspanish.com/index.htm

MUSIC

The study of Music offers you the opportunity to develop your performing, composing and listening skills.

GCSE Music

Clearly, an interest in music is a key factor in deciding whether GCSE Music is for you. The wider the range of your musical interests the better. However, you need to be aware that the course will be about much more than listening to, singing or playing music. There is a lot of practical work, but there is also a lot of hard work, some of it of a more theoretical nature. You will need to be well organised and will probably need to develop several key skills such as problem solving and being able to work well in a team.

The course involves both practical work and theory. You will be involved in performing, composing, listening and learning to appreciate music. You will also learn to develop skills as a musician or singer.

Main elements of the course

The outline below is based on what the majority of exam board syllabuses include. For an exact description of the syllabus you will be studying, you will need to contact your school or the exam board itself.

You can expect to study:

- personal performance
- musical relationships
- role of voices and instruments
- music appreciation
- music for dance
- technical elements of music (devices, instrumentation, melody and harmony, notation, rhythm and metre, and texture).

How is Music taught and assessed?

Teacher-led activity is likely to include the technical study of the way music is made up, the history of music, and the study of various genres of music, including:

- choral and a cappella singing
- classical
- film
- jazz
- pop ballads
- contemporary, including rapping
- world music.

There is plenty of practical work too, particularly involving playing, singing and listening.

Assessment may be up to 60% controlled assessment (e.g. solo performing, ensemble performing, musical composition), plus written tests or examination. Part of the written examination might be to listen to a CD and answer questions that draw on several topics studied during the course.

Music at A level

An A level in Music will offer you the opportunity to further develop your performing, composing and listening skills. The course will also introduce you to a wide variety of music. The course will include the following elements:

- composing
- history of music
- listening comprehension
- performance
- understanding the mechanics of music.

There is also an A level in Music Technology. There is some overlap with A level Music, but here the emphasis is always on how technology is used in relation to the range of musical genres, traditions or styles. There is also a greater emphasis on analysing modern popular music.

Music and choosing a career

If you are thinking of earning a living through music, you need to be aware that many areas of the work are extremely competitive and very high-level skills are therefore necessary. Some performers work semi-professionally, that is, they typically do a second job in the evening or at weekends to help increase their income.

Examples of jobs and careers in music include: composer, disc jockey, music therapist, musical instrument maker/repairer, music journalist, musician, private music teacher, promotion assistant or manager, and singer. For many of these jobs a degree is at least helpful, although still not a guarantee in a very popular occupational sector.

Further information

- BBC GCSE Bitesize   www.bbc.co.uk/schools/gcsebitesize/music
- BBC Music   www.bbc.co.uk/music
- British Society for Music Therapy   www.bsmt.org
- Catalogue of Internet Resources   http://bubl.ac.uk/link/m/musiceducation.htm
- The MusicLand   www.themusicland.co.uk
- Music at School   www.musicatschool.co.uk
- Shillam, Tania, *Music Industry Uncovered*, Trotman
- *Working in Music*, VT Lifeskills

PHYSICAL EDUCATION (PE)

PE covers many areas, including health and exercise, sport and recreation. It develops the competence and confidence to take part in different physical activities and learn about the value of a healthy, active lifestyle. Students of PE develop a wide range of skills and the ability to use tactics and strategies, and to develop ideas to perform successfully.

GCSE Physical Education

Although there is an obvious appeal for students who have already discovered that they have outstanding talent in aspects of sport or PE, the subject is not exclusively for them. It is likely to appeal to anyone with an interest in physical activity and performance. You learn how to exercise safely and effectively to improve health and well-being.

Main elements of the course

The outline below is based on what the majority of exam board syllabuses include. For an exact description of the syllabus you will be studying, you will need to contact your school or the exam board itself.

A GCSE in PE involves the study of topics across the full range of physical education, including:

- active and healthy lifestyles
- anatomy and physiology
- developing skills and techniques
- physical and mental capacity
- evaluating and improving
- safety and risk assessment
- training and performance.

Practical skills are developed from a very wide range of activities, including:

- archery
- athletics
- badminton
- basketball
- cricket
- football (soccer)
- hockey
- netball
- outdoor and adventure activities
- rugby
- water sports.

Short course

There is also a short course GCSE available in this subject. The short course is both a 'stand-alone' qualification and also serves as the first half of the full course GCSE. The short course is assessed at the same standard as the full GCSE course and is made up of two compulsory units. The course takes half the time allocated to the full course GCSE.

See also the introduction to short courses on page 8.

How is PE taught and assessed?

You should expect some formal teaching – for example, about decision-making and tactics, the rules of particular sports, anatomy and physiology – as well as plenty of practical work in and around your chosen sporting activities.

You will be assessed during the course and in the final practical assessment on your performance in your selected activities. You will also learn how to assess and analyse the performance of others. For both the full and short courses, 60% of the marks are awarded for controlled assessment (including the assessment of performance) and 40% for the exam.

PE at A level

In A level PE you learn about specific physical activities and develop the skills of planning, performing and evaluating these activities. You also gain an insight into the historical and social context of sport, as well as the relationship between psychology and physiology in sport.

The main elements of the course are likely to include:

- the social basis of sport and recreation
- enhancing performance
- principles and methods of exercise and training
- comparative investigation of sport and recreation.

PE and choosing a career

There is more variation in entry level in this occupational sector than with many others. It is possible to get into some sports-related areas without A levels (or equivalent), although having a qualification is usually an advantage. Work in leisure clubs and gyms, for example as an assistant, health and fitness instructor or swimming pool attendant, may be available at this level.

You usually need a combination of sporting prowess and suitable qualifications to take up a job in coaching and personal training. Having a degree (or equivalent) is becoming increasingly necessary in jobs such as fitness or leisure centre manager, outdoor pursuits manager, physiotherapist, sports administrator, sports development officer and sports therapist.

Further information

- BBC GCSE Bitesize   www.bbc.co.uk/schools/gcsebitesize/pe

- BBC Health   www.bbc.co.uk/health

- BBC Science and Nature –   www.bbc.co.uk/science/humanbody
  Human Body and Mind

- British Association of Sport   www.bases.org.uk
  and Exercise Sciences

- PE Centre GCSE   www.physicaleducation.co.uk/GCSE/gcse.htm

- S-Cool PE GCSE   www.s-cool.co.uk/gcse/pe

- Sport England   www.sportengland.org

- UK Sport   www.uksport.gov.uk

- Dixon, Beryl, *Sport and Fitness Uncovered*, Trotman

PHYSICS

Physics is the study of how the physical world works. It helps us to:

- learn how scientific work is evaluated, published and verified by the scientific community
- understand how physics is used in the modern world
- explore the properties of motion, nuclear physics, energy transfer and electricity
- develop better awareness of how advances in science and technology affect the world.

Note: The new specifications for GCSEs in all science subjects will start in September 2012.

GCSE Physics

GCSE Physics is one of three separate science awards (the others are Biology and Chemistry) that together cover the requirements of the Key Stage 4 programme of study. You can also combine the study of these three subjects in a GCSE Science and/or Additional Science course (see separate entry for GCSE Science).

GCSE Physics takes the physics from GCSE Science and the physics from GCSE Additional Science and adds a bit more to form a qualification that is wholly Physics. If you study in a state-maintained school, it will be compulsory for you to do the complete programme of study, so you will be required to follow courses in all three separate sciences if you take this pathway.

The main advantage of taking the single sciences separately is that you can keep open a wider range of scientific career routes.

Main elements of the course

The outline below is based on what the majority of exam board syllabuses include. For an exact description of the syllabus you will be studying, you will need to contact your school or the exam board itself.

The main topics in a GCSE Physics course are:

- electricity
- forces and motion
- radiation
- radioactivity
- the characteristics of waves
- the Earth, solar system, stars and the universe.

How is Physics taught and assessed?

You will be taught how to:

- recognise, recall and show understanding of specific scientific facts, terms, principles, ideas and practical techniques

- show understanding of the power and limitations of scientific ideas, and the things that affect how these ideas develop
- use your knowledge to show understanding of the benefits and drawbacks of applications of science
- apply your knowledge and understanding by analysis and evaluation of information and data
- apply investigative methods (that is, do experiments), including practical techniques that require skill.

The style and weightings of assessment vary depending on the syllabus, but each scheme of assessment includes a final exam.

Physics at A level

A level Physics is intended to help you understand how the physical world works and to establish links between theory and experiment. The main elements of the course are:

- electricity and thermal physics
- forces and fields
- materials
- mechanics and radioactivity
- nuclear and particle physics
- patterns and particle accelerators
- wave physics.

Physics and choosing a career

Taking one or more of the separate sciences as a GCSE is the best way of preparing for an A level in the same subject. For most jobs where you will be making direct use of physics, you need to be thinking in terms of at least a first degree. Some forms of work as a laboratory technician would be a possibility with A levels or a suitable Diploma or BTEC National.

Graduate jobs related to physics include: electronics engineer, geoscientist, materials engineer, medical physicist, meteorologist, research scientist, and scientific laboratory technician.

Further information

- BBC Science and Nature   www.bbc.co.uk/sn
- BrainPOP   www.brainpop.com
- Catalogue of Internet Resources   http://bubl.ac.uk/link/p/physicseducation.htm
- Fear of Physics   www.fearofphysics.com
- Institute of Physics   www.iop.org
- Physics and Astronomy online   www.physlink.com
- Sparknotes – Physics   www.sparknotes.com/physics/

RELIGIOUS STUDIES

Religious Studies looks at the purpose of life and the basic moral, philosophical and spiritual questions that anyone can have. You will study the various systems of beliefs that have at their centre a belief in the existence of a God or gods.

GCSE Religious Studies

Religious Studies is not only for students who have a religious faith of some sort. It explores a range of religious beliefs and experience and looks at the place of religion in the world of today.

The course will develop your knowledge and understanding of Christianity and one or two of the following religions: Buddhism, Hinduism, Islam, Judaism and Sikhism. It will also introduce you to important moral, philosophical and spiritual questions, and help you develop the skills to deal with them.

Main elements of the course

The outline below is based on what the majority of exam board syllabuses include. For an exact description of the syllabus you will be studying, you will need to contact your school or the exam board itself.

The topics studied will include some of the following:

- death and the afterlife
- religion and equality, prejudice and discrimination
- religion and human relationships
- religion and medical ethics
- religion, peace and justice
- religion, poverty and wealth
- religion, science and the environment
- sanctity of life
- the concepts of good and evil
- the nature of God
- war and peace.

Variations

Religious Studies: World Religion

Both full and short courses are available in this GCSE. The specification includes six religions, and you will have the option to focus on one of the three major world religions (Christianity, Islam and Judaism) throughout or to study a combination of two or three different religions (the three major religions plus Buddhism, Sikhism and Hinduism).

Religious Studies: Philosophy and Applied Ethics
Both full and short courses are available in this GCSE. In this course you will investigate issue-based topics that are not restricted to one particular faith or background. There is, however, reference to the faith and context of the major religions.

Religion and Belief in Today's World
Both full and short courses are available in this GCSE. You will study several topics relating to religion and beliefs in the modern world, with reference to the major religions practised in Britain.

See also the introduction to short courses on page 8.

How is Religious Studies taught and assessed?

Assessment in Religious Studies is now entirely through examination.

Religious Studies at A level

A level Religious Studies considers the fundamental questions of human existence, examining issues such as the interaction between religion and science. The main elements of the course are likely to include:

- developments in Christian thought
- other world religions, including Islam, Judaism, Buddhism and/or Hinduism
- philosophy of religion
- religious ethics
- religious texts, including Jewish scriptures and the New Testament.

Religious Studies and choosing a career

There are few jobs directly related to Religious Studies below degree level. Becoming a minister of religion or a teacher of religious studies are the most clearly related graduate career options Other jobs that might benefit from a religious studies background include charity worker, counsellor, foreign affairs journalist, police officer, religious worker or leader, social worker, or youth and community worker.

Further information

- BBC GCSE Bitesize   www.bbc.co.uk/schools/gcsebitesize/rs

- BBC Religion   www.bbc.co.uk/religion

- Catalogue of Internet Resources   http://bubl.ac.uk/link/r/religiouseducation.htm

- Church of England   www.cofe.anglican.org

- Council of Christians and Jews   www.ccj.org.uk

- Hinduism for Schools   www.hinduism.fsnet.co.uk

- Interfaith   www.interfaith.org

- Introduction to Sikhism   www.sikhs.org/summary.htm

- Islamic Foundation   www.islamic-foundation.org.uk

- Judaism 101   www.jewfaq.org/index.htm

- National Society for Promoting   www.natsoc.org.uk
  Religious Education

SCIENCE

Science is the field of study which attempts to describe and understand the nature of the universe. The government takes the view that everyone needs a basic understanding of science and technology. Science is therefore a compulsory subject at Key Stage 4. However, the traditional approach to science does not suit everyone and the government has consequently encouraged the development of a range of courses at Key Stage 4.

GCSEs in Science

The GCSE Science criteria have been the last subject criteria to be reviewed in the ongoing reform process. From September 2011, all new Key Stage 4 learners will follow the new GCSE syllabuses.

GCSE qualifications in the sciences are designed to meet two quite different needs: firstly, to prepare all students for their future roles as consumers and citizens in the 21st century, in which science is a part of everyday experience, and, secondly, to prepare future scientists for specialist science studies at A level and beyond.

Changes to the statutory programme of study for Key Stage 4 in recent years have placed greater emphasis on the nature of science – 'how science works'. Most students will take one or more GCSEs in this subject area. The main options are:

- GCSE Science, taken on its own
- GCSE Science and GCSE Additional Science (two separate GCSEs)
- GCSE Applied Science – a Double Award which is worth two GCSEs
- the three science GCSEs (Biology, Chemistry and Physics) taken separately.

Main elements of the course
The outline below is based on what the majority of exam board syllabuses include in the range of courses. For an exact description of the syllabus you will be studying, you will need to contact your school or the exam board itself.

GCSE Science
GCSE Science aims to develop scientific literacy. The two main areas of study are:

- key science explanations – which help us to make sense of our lives
- ideas about science – which show how science works.

The core topics in GCSE Science are Biology, Chemistry and Physics (see entries for these as separate subjects to read about the kinds of topics you can expect to cover).

GCSE Additional Science
GCSE Additional Science builds on GCSE Science to help you acquire the knowledge, understanding and skills needed for future study – to AS and A levels (or the equivalent) and beyond in engineering, medicine or other fields of science.

GCSE Applied Science
Applied Science is a Double Award GCSE and will appeal to you if you want to find out more about how science meets the needs of society and if you have an interest in the practical application of science. You will learn how science is used in everyday life and the importance of standardised procedures, and how to apply them in problem solving. There is a strong focus on work-related learning. You will develop the practical scientific capability needed for jobs in, for example, health care, agriculture, manufacturing, communications and technical quality assurance.

GCSEs in Biology, Chemistry and Physics
See the separate descriptions of these subjects elsewhere in this part of the book (in the sections Biology, Chemistry and Physics, respectively).

Other variations
- Rural and Agricultural Science
- Environmental and Land-based Science

How is Science taught and assessed?

There is considerable variation between the different syllabuses and the way they are taught. However, you can expect to learn about the relationships between data, evidence, theories and explanations, and develop your practical and enquiry skills. You will also learn to communicate your ideas with clarity and precision. Other topics in the course include the applications and implications of science in the modern world. You will develop the knowledge, understanding and skills that you require if you wish to pursue further studies in science and related areas.

The Science courses assessment weightings vary. Between 25% and 75% of the marks can be allocated to controlled assessment, and the rest of the assessment is by examination. All Science GCSEs are Single Awards except for Applied Science, which is a Double Award.

Applied Science at A level

The emphasis, as in GCSE Applied Science, is on learning about how science is applied in practical ways, in business, in research or in any other way that affects people's lives. The main elements are:

- analysis
- energy
- evaluation of the investigation
- health and safety in organisations using science

- health science
- planning and carrying out an investigation
- practical techniques and procedures
- processing and presenting data in investigation
- science and the community
- study of organisations using science.

Science and choosing a career

Read the information given in each individual science (Biology, Chemistry, Physics) section. Many jobs need science subjects and taking just a single science subject may limit your job or career options, so you do need to think about your choices very carefully.

Further information

- BBC Science and Nature   www.bbc.co.uk/sn

- BrainPOP   www.brainpop.com

- Catalogue of Internet Resources   http://bubl.ac.uk/link/s/scienceeducationuk.htm

- Forensic Science Society   www.forensic-science-society.org.uk

- Institute of Biomedical Science   www.ibms.org

- Institute of Physics   www.iop.org

- NHS Careers   www.nhscareers.nhs.uk

- Royal Society of Chemistry   www.rsc.org/Education/index.asp

CHAPTER FIVE

Diplomas

What subjects are available in the Diploma?

The Diploma is available at three different levels. Levels 1 and 2 are the levels that are normally available at Key Stage 4. You can select whichever level Diploma suits you best.

- Level 1: equivalent in size and status to four to five GCSEs at grades D–G.
- Level 2: equivalent in size and status to five to six GCSEs at grades A*–C.

The Diploma will not take up all of your time at Key Stage 4. You will also study some elements of the National Curriculum, probably including GCSEs.

From September 2010, Diploma courses will be available in 14 subject areas:

- Business, Administration and Finance
- Construction and the Built Environment
- Creative and Media
- Engineering
- Environmental and Land-based Studies
- Hair and Beauty Studies
- Hospitality
- Information Technology
- Manufacturing and Product Design
- Public Services
- Retail Business
- Society, Health and Development
- Sport and Active Leisure
- Travel and Tourism.

Three further subject areas are to be launched in September 2011:

- Humanities and Social Sciences
- Languages and International communication
- Science (where Advanced Lavel will not be available until 2012).

Directory of Diplomas

The following pages give more detailed information about each of these Diplomas. Each subject or learning line is discussed using the following:

- overview of the subject area
- the various levels of Diploma

- main areas of learning (**principal**, **additional/specialist** and **generic**)
- how the Diploma is taught and assessed
- the next step from the particular Diploma
- the Diploma and choosing a career pathway.

Syllabus information

If you need more information on any particular Diploma that interests you, it's a good idea to check out the syllabus of the relevant exam board that your school or college runs. These can be found on the exam board websites, which are listed below.

AS/A levels, Advanced Diplomas and equivalents

A levels and Advanced Diplomas will provide the main progression routes if you want to go on to university and/or high status careers. However, there are some excellent alternatives, such as the International Baccalaureate (offered by some schools and sixth form colleges) and BTEC and OCR Nationals (usually offered in colleges of further education).

The availability of courses in a particular subject area at A level, Advanced Diploma and BTEC or OCR National is listed in each subject section.

Future careers

Each subject area includes ideas for possible future careers.

What to do next

As you browse through the subject entries, try to have in mind the following questions.

- Would I enjoy studying this Diploma?
- Would I do well in this Diploma learning line, given the type of assessment methods used?
- How would choosing this Diploma affect my plans for further study ay 16+?
- How would choosing this subject affect my career options?

If you are still finding it difficult to choose between a few subjects, look again at Chapter Three, 'Choosing Your Subjects', in Part One (page 23).

BUSINESS, ADMINISTRATION AND FINANCE

The Diploma in Business, Administration and Finance uses a mix of theoretical and applied learning approaches to teach you about business enterprise, business administration and finance.

Foundation and Higher Diplomas

The Foundation Diploma is equivalent to five GCSEs at grades D–G. The Higher Diploma is equivalent to seven GCSEs at grades A*–C.

Your teachers and advisers will be able to help you decide which level is more appropriate for you at this stage of your learning.

How is the Diploma in Business, Administration and Finance taught and assessed?

In the principal learning element, you will learn about the issues that affect business today, how it works and what skills you need to have. This will include:

- business enterprise: developing ideas, carrying out research and promoting products or services
- business administration: learning about business administration and how important it is to organisations
- finance: acquiring the knowledge and skills you need to manage personal and business finances.

You will also do a minimum of 10 days' work experience and get the chance to learn from people working in business.

At each level, you can develop your particular business, administration and finance interests further by taking specialist courses relating to your chosen subject and career ambitions. For example, you could learn more about ICT or human resources. Alternatively, you can choose subjects that would help you get into university, such as law and statistics. You could also broaden your learning by studying a different subject altogether, perhaps a foreign language, a humanities subject, music or science.

During the course, you will also complete a student project to demonstrate the skills and knowledge you have learned, for example on aspects of customer provision or satisfaction.

As part of your generic learning, you also continue to study English, Maths and ICT but you will study these subjects particularly for their relevance to the business sector. You also learn teamwork, self-management and presentation skills, and how to apply your knowledge and skills creatively in a business environment.

Advanced Level

The Advanced Level Diploma is normally taken in the sixth form or in a college of further education. It is equivalent to three and a half A levels and is worth 420 UCAS points.

There is also a Progression Level Diploma, which is like the Advanced Diploma, but without various options, and it is equivalent to two A levels. It is worth 300 UCAS points.

From 2011, an Extended Diploma will also be available, which will include more generic, as well as additional and specialist, learning.

After doing the Progression, Advanced or Extended Diploma you could go on to college or university, or to further training and employment.

The Diploma in Business, Administration and Finance and choosing a career

A Diploma in Business, Administration and Finance does not mean you have to take up a career in this sector. The Diploma gives you a wide range of next-step options. After studying a Foundation or Higher Diploma in Business, Administration and Finance, you might choose to do a Progression, Advanced or Extended Diploma, or perhaps do A levels. You could also do an Apprenticeship or take up a job with further training. For ideas on specific careers in business, administration and finance, look at the careers pathway section on page 46.

Further information

- Business, Administration and   www.baf-diploma.org.uk
  Finance Diploma website

- BBC Business   www.bbc.co.uk/business

- Bank of England   www.bankofengland.co.uk

- biz/ed   www.bized.co.uk

- Business Studies Online   www.businessstudiesonline.co.uk

- Council for Administration – Careers   www.breakinto.biz

- Investing for Kids   http://library.thinkquest.org/3096

- The Times 100   www.thetimes100.co.uk

- Young Enterprise   www.young-enterprise.org.uk

- *How to Get Ahead In …Business and Finance*, Raintree

CONSTRUCTION AND THE BUILT ENVIRONMENT

The Diploma in Construction and the Built Environment uses a mix of theoretical and applied learning approaches to help you gain an understanding of the construction industry and to develop the skills which employers in this sector are seeking. This sector includes industries such as architecture, structural steelwork, heating and ventilation, painting and decorating, and surveying.

Foundation and Higher Diplomas

The Foundation Diploma is equivalent to five GCSEs at grades D–G. The Higher Diploma is equivalent to seven GCSEs at grades A*–C.

Your teachers and advisers will be able to help you decide which level is more appropriate for you at this stage of your learning.

How is the Diploma in Construction and the Built Environment taught and assessed?

The principal learning element includes:

- understanding how the built environment is designed and constructed, how it impacts on people and communities, and how history, politics and economics affect it
- developing a range of skills and knowledge needed in different industries – for example, using tools and understanding modern construction methods and materials
- analysing the need for good management and continuous maintenance
- understanding the importance of good design, workmanship and teamwork.

You will also do a minimum of 10 days' work experience and get the chance to learn from professionals in the sector.

You can choose another option or specialist learning options to meet your personal interests and career goals. You could, for example, choose specialist courses that relate to your chosen subject and career ambitions, such as plumbing or joinery. You could choose to learn about housing or the impact different kinds of land use has on the safety, health and well-being of communities. Alternatively, you could broaden your learning by studying a different subject altogether, perhaps a foreign language, a humanities subject or music.

During the course, you will also complete a student project to demonstrate the skills and knowledge you have been able to develop, for example on the design of a new building or structure.

As part of your generic learning, you will also continue to study English, Maths and ICT. But you will study these subjects particularly for their relevance to construction and the built environment. You also learn teamwork, self-management and presentation skills, and how to apply your knowledge and skills creatively in a business environment.

Advanced Level

The Advanced Level Diploma is normally taken in the sixth form or in a college of further education. It is equivalent to three and a half A levels and is worth 420 UCAS points.

There is also a Progression Level Diploma, which is like the Advanced Diploma, but without various options, and it is equivalent to two A levels. It is worth 300 UCAS points.

From 2011, an Extended Diploma will also be available, which will have more generic, as well as additional and specialist, learning.

After doing the Progression, Advanced or Extended Diploma you could go on to college or university, or to further training and employment.

The Diploma in Construction and the Built Environment and choosing a career

A Diploma in Construction and the Built Environment does not mean you have to take up a career in this sector. The Diploma is designed to give you a wide range of next-step options. After studying a Foundation or Higher Diploma in Construction and the Built Environment, you might choose to do a Progression, Advanced or Extended Diploma, or perhaps do A levels. You could also start an Apprenticeship or take up a job with further training. If you do want a career in the specific sector, you might choose to aim for a university degree in construction management, building services engineering, housing practice, planning or architecture. Alternatively, you could consider a career as a building services contractor, construction worker, electrician, engineer, urban planner, property developer, estate agent, or restorer of old buildings.

Further information

- Construction and the Built   www.cbediploma.co.uk/employers
  Environment Diploma website

- Chartered Institute of   www.ciat.org.uk/en/careers
  Architectural Technologists

- Chartered Institute of Plumbing   www.ciphe.org.uk/Professional/Careers
  and Heating Engineering

- Chartered Institution of   www.cibse.org
  Building Services Engineers

- Construction Skills   www.constructionskills.net

- Construction Youth Trust   www.constructionyouth.org.uk

- Institution of Civil Engineering Surveyors www.ices.org.uk/careers.php

- Institution of Structural Engineers www.istructe.org

- Landscape Institute www.landscapeinstitute.org/education

- Royal Institute of British Architects www.architecture.com/EducationAndCareers/BecomingAnArchitect/

- Pilgrim, Dee, *Real Life Guide to Construction*, Trotman

- Ryder, Tim and Penrith, Deborah, *Working with the Environment*, Vocation Work

CREATIVE AND MEDIA

The Diploma in Creative and Media uses a mix of theoretical and applied learning approaches to help you gain knowledge and understanding about the creative industries, which include dance, drama, fashion, film, music, publishing, and television. A full list of sector-related disciplines is listed under the heading 'How is the Diploma in Creative and Media taught and assessed?'

Foundation and Higher Diplomas

The Foundation Diploma is equivalent to five GCSEs at grades D–G. The Higher Diploma is equivalent to seven GCSEs at grades A*–C.

Your teachers and advisers will be able to help you decide which level is more appropriate for you at this stage of your learning.

How is the Diploma in Creative and Media taught and assessed?

The principal learning element includes the various disciplines that make up Creative and Media. The content is delivered via four themes:

- creativity in context
- thinking and working creatively
- principles, processes and practice
- creative businesses and enterprise.

These four themes are applied in the study of one or more of the various sector-related disciplines. These include two- and three-dimensional visual art, craft, graphic design, product design, fashion, textiles, footwear, advertising, drama, dance, film, music, television, audio and radio, interactive media, animation, computer games, photo imaging and creative writing.

You will also do a minimum of 10 days' work experience and get the chance to learn from professionals. This does not have to be related to one of the creative and media areas of work.

You can choose other additional or specialist learning options to meet your personal interests and career goals. You could, for example, choose to cover a particular creative and media-related topic in greater depth. Alternatively, you could broaden your learning by studying a different subject altogether, perhaps a foreign language, a humanities subject, or a science.

During the course, you will also complete a project, building up an evidence portfolio that will demonstrate the skills and knowledge you have been able to develop in relation to one of the sector-related disciplines or a combination of two or three of these disciplines.

As part of your generic learning, you also continue with the learning of English, Maths and ICT but these subjects are taught particularly for their relevance to the creative and media sector. You also learn teamwork, self-management and presentation skills, and how to apply your knowledge and skills creatively in a business environment.

Advanced Level

The Advanced Level Diploma is normally taken in the sixth form or in a college of further education. It is equivalent to three and a half A levels and is worth 420 UCAS points.

There is also a Progression Level Diploma, which is like the Advanced Diploma, but without various options, and it is equivalent to two A levels. It is worth 300 UCAS points.

From 2011, an Extended Diploma will also be available, which will have more generic, as well as additional and specialist, learning.

After doing the Progression, Advanced or Extended Diploma you could go on to college or university, or to further training and employment.

The Diploma in Creative and Media and choosing a career

A Diploma in Creative and Media does not mean you have to take up a career in this sector. The Diploma is designed to give you a wide range of next-step options. After studying a Foundation or Higher Diploma in Creative and Media, you might choose to do a Progression, Advanced or Extended Diploma, or perhaps do A levels. You could also do an Apprenticeship or take up a job with further training. For ideas on specific careers in the creative and media sector, you could look at the careers pathway section on page 40 and also investigate careers in any of the related disciplines mentioned in this section.

Further information

- Creative and Media Diploma website   www.skillset.org/qualifications/diploma/

- Catalogue of Internet Resources   http://bubl.ac.uk/link/m/mediastudies.htm

- Creative and Cultural Skills   www.creative-choices.co.uk

- Skillfast-UK (Sector Skills Council for Fashion and Media)   www.skillfast-uk.org/justthejob

- Skillset (the Sector Skills Council for Creative Media)   www.skillset.org/careers

- Holmes, Karen, *Real Life Guide to Creative Industries*, Trotman

- Miller, Rose and Zajac, Camilla, *Real Life Guide to Hospitality and Events Management*, Trotman

ENGINEERING

The Diploma in Engineering uses a mix of theoretical and applied learning approaches to help you use your maths, science, technology and creative skills in designing and making products.

Foundation and Higher Diplomas

The Foundation Diploma is equivalent to five GCSEs at grades D–G. The Higher Diploma is equivalent to seven GCSEs at grades A*–C.

Your teachers and advisers will be able to help you decide which level is more appropriate for you at this stage of your learning.

How is the Diploma in Engineering taught and assessed?

The principal learning element includes:

- basic engineering principles
- the importance and impact of engineering on our lives
- what makes innovations succeed, how new materials contribute to design, how to develop and launch new ideas.

You will also do a minimum of 10 days' engineering work experience and get the chance to learn from professional engineers.

You can choose other additional or specialist learning options to meet your personal interests and career goals. You could, for example, choose to study engineering topics such as robotics, medical engineering or aerospace. Alternatively, you could broaden your learning by studying a different subject altogether, perhaps a foreign language, a humanities subject, music or science.

During the course, you will also complete a practical project as evidence of the skills and knowledge you will have developed, for example, a project on the contribution that engineering can make to improving the lives of people with disabilities.

As part of your generic learning, you will continue to study English, Maths and ICT but you will study these subjects particularly for their relevance to engineering. You will also learn teamwork, self-management and presentation skills, and how to apply your knowledge and skills creatively in a business environment.

Advanced Level

The Advanced Level Diploma is normally taken in the sixth form or in a college of further education. It is equivalent to three and a half A levels and is worth 420 UCAS points.

There is also a Progression Level Diploma, which is like the Advanced Diploma, but without various options, and it is equivalent to two A levels. It is worth 300 UCAS points.

From 2011, an Extended Diploma will also be available, which will have more generic, as well as additional and specialist, learning.

After doing the Progression, Advanced or Extended Diploma you could go on to college or university, or to further training and employment.

The Diploma in Engineering and choosing a career

A Diploma in Engineering does not mean you have to take up a career in this sector. The Diploma is designed to give you a wide range of next-step options. After studying a Foundation or Higher Diploma in Engineering, you might choose to do a Progression, Advanced or Extended Diploma, or perhaps do A levels. You could also do an Apprenticeship or take up a job with further training. For ideas on specific careers in engineering, look at the careers pathway section on page 60.

Further information

- Engineering Diploma website   www.engineeringdiploma.com

- Catalogue of Internet Resources   http://bubl.ac.uk/link/e/engineeringeducation.htm

- Why Study Materials?   www.whystudymaterials.ac.uk

- Garner, Geraldine, *Careers in Engineering*, McGraw-Hill

- *How to Get Ahead In … Engineering and Design*, Raintree

ENVIRONMENTAL AND LAND-BASED STUDIES

The Diploma in Environmental and Land-based Studies uses a mix of theoretical and applied learning approaches to help you understand and study environmental and land-based subjects.

Foundation and Higher Diplomas

The Foundation Diploma is equivalent to five GCSEs at grades D–G. The Higher Diploma is equivalent to seven GCSEs at grades A*–C.

Your teachers and advisers will be able to help you decide which level is more appropriate for you at this stage of your learning.

How is the Diploma in Environmental and Land-based Studies taught and assessed?

The principal learning element covers three main areas:

- the limited resources of our natural environment, our impact on it, how it influences us and how these resources are used
- how we use plants for commercial, recreational and conservation purposes and animals for production (food), recreation, work or companionship
- the impact we have on our environment and how important it is to use environmentally friendly 'green' practices.

You will learn to have proper consideration of health and safety and you will develop scientific, communication and management skills. You will also develop entrepreneurial and creative skills, a preparation for the possibility of eventually running your own business in this area.

You will also do fieldwork to study different habitats and you will do a minimum of 10 days' work experience, getting the chance to learn by working with professionals.

You can choose other additional or specialist learning options to meet your personal interests and career goals. You could, for example, choose to study in greater depth topics that are related to the environment. Alternatively, you could broaden your learning by studying a different subject altogether, perhaps a foreign language, history or music.

During the course, you will also complete a practical project as evidence of the skills and knowledge you would have developed, for example on an aspect of the human 'carbon footprint'.

As part of your generic learning, you will also continue to study English, Maths and ICT but you will study these subjects particularly for their relevance to Environmental and Land-based Studies. You also learn teamwork, self-management and presentation skills, and how to apply your knowledge and skills creatively in a business environment.

Advanced Level

The Advanced Level Diploma is normally taken in the sixth form or in a college of further education. It is equivalent to three and a half A levels and is worth 420 UCAS points.

There is also a Progression Level Diploma, which is like the Advanced Diploma, but without various options, and it is equivalent to two A levels. It is worth 300 UCAS points.

From 2011, an Extended Diploma will also be available, which will have more generic, as well as additional and specialist, learning.

After doing the Progression, Advanced or Extended Diploma you could go on to college or university, or to further training and employment.

The Diploma in Environmental and Land-based Studies and choosing a career

A Diploma in Environmental and Land-based Studies does not mean you have to take up a career in this broad area of work. The Diploma is designed to give you a wide range of next-step options. After studying a Foundation or Higher Diploma in Environmental and Land-based Studies, you might choose to do a Progression, Advanced or Extended Diploma, or perhaps do A levels. You could also do an Apprenticeship or take up a job with further training. Specific careers that do relate to Environmental and Land-based Studies include animal protection and other work with animals, agriculture, arboriculture, charity work, fish farming, forestry, grounds maintenance and greenkeeping, horticulture, and landscape gardening.

Further information

- Environmental and Land-based   www.diplomaelbs.co.uk
  Studies Diploma website

- Department for the Environment,   www.defra.gov.uk
  Food and Rural Affairs

- Farming and Countryside Education   www.face-online.org.uk

- Institute of Biology   www.societyofbiology.org/education

- Lantra (the Sector Skills Council for   www.lantra.co.uk/young-people-and-parents
  Environmental and Land-based industries)

- Natural England   www.naturalengland.org.uk

- The Wildlife Trusts   www.wildlifetrusts.org

HAIR AND BEAUTY STUDIES

The Diploma in Hair and Beauty Studies uses a mix of theoretical and practical learning approaches to help you learn about working in the hair and beauty sector. The sector is made up of six industries: hairdressing, barbering, African Caribbean hairdressing and barbering, beauty therapy, spa therapy and nail services.

Foundation and Higher Diplomas

The Foundation Diploma is equivalent to five GCSEs at grades D–G. The Higher Diploma is equivalent to seven GCSEs at grades A*–C.

Your teachers and advisers will be able to help you decide which level is more appropriate for you at this stage of your learning.

How is the Diploma in Hair and Beauty Studies taught and assessed?

The principal learning element includes:

- principles of basic hair, beauty and nail treatments and routines
- the global environment in which hair and beauty businesses operate
- the influence of personality, culture, race, gender, fashion and religion
- research and innovation in hair and beauty product design
- personal presentation, hygiene and well-being
- communication skills, including customer relations
- promotion and selling
- business systems and processes involved in running a salon, barbershop, nail bar or spa.

You will also do a minimum of 10 days' work experience and get the chance to learn from professionals in the sector, perhaps in a hairdresser's salon, a spa centre or at a make-up counter.

You can choose other additional or specialist learning options to meet your personal interests and career goals. You could, for example, learn to plait or twist hair, learn themed face painting or study complementary and alternative health therapies. Alternatively, you could broaden your learning by taking an additional science subject that might help you with your principal learning. You could also pick a different subject altogether, perhaps a foreign language, a humanities subject or music.

During the course, you will also complete a practical project as evidence of the skills and knowledge you would have developed. It could be a written piece of work, a piece of research or something practical, such as a video on the different hairstyles and looks you find in a culturally diverse area.

As part of your generic learning, you also continue with the learning of English, Maths and ICT but these subjects are taught particularly for their relevance to Hair and Beauty Studies. You also learn teamwork, self-management and presentation skills, and how to apply your knowledge and skills creatively in a business environment.

Advanced Level

The Advanced Level Diploma is normally taken in the sixth form or in a college of further education. It is equivalent to three and a half A levels and is worth 420 UCAS points.

There is also a Progression Level Diploma, which is like the Advanced Diploma, but without various options, and it is equivalent to two A levels. It is worth 300 UCAS points.

From 2011, an Extended Diploma will also be available, which will have more generic, as well as additional and specialist, learning.

After doing the Progression, Advanced or Extended Diploma you could go on to college or university, or to further training and employment.

The Diploma in Hair and Beauty Studies and choosing a career

A Diploma in Hair and Beauty Studies does not mean you have to take up a career in this sector. The Diploma is designed to give you a wide range of next-step options. After studying a Foundation or Higher Diploma in Hair and Beauty Studies, you might choose to do a Progression, Advanced or Extended Diploma, or perhaps do A levels. You could also do an Apprenticeship or take up a job with further training. Careers that are directly related to Hair and Beauty Studies include beauty consultant, body artist/tattooist, hairdresser/barber, make-up artist, nail technician, spa centre therapist, store demonstrator and wigmaker.

Further information

• Hair and Beauty Diploma website	www.habia.org/diploma
• British Association of Beauty Therapy and Cosmetology	www.babtac.com
• Complementary Therapists Association	www.complementary.assoc.org.uk/Quals/?QC=29
• Guild of Professional Beauty Therapists	www.beautyguild.com
• Hairdressing and Beauty Industry Authority	www.habia.org
• Institute of Trichologists	www.trichologists.org.uk/about.htm
• Skillset (Sector Skills Council for Creative and Media)	www.skillset.org
• Tattoo Club of Great Britain	www.tattoo.co.uk

HOSPITALITY

The Diploma in Hospitality uses a mix of theoretical and applied learning approaches to introduce you to the hospitality industry and customer service. It helps you develop the skills to work in the industry, e.g. in preparing and serving food and drink.

Foundation and Higher Diplomas

The Foundation Diploma is equivalent to five GCSEs at grades D–G. The Higher Diploma is equivalent to seven GCSEs at grades A*–C.

Your teachers and advisers will be able to help you decide on which level is more appropriate for you at this stage of your learning.

How is the Diploma in Hospitality taught and assessed?

The principal learning element includes:

- learning about the hospitality industry and the different departments that make up a hospitality business
- what's involved in running a restaurant, café or hotel
- developing the skills you need to work in the industry
- financial aspects, including pricing and budgeting
- customer service
- basic legislation and health and safety.

You will also do a minimum of 10 days' engineering work experience and get the chance to learn from professionals in the industry, e.g. taking a placement in an events company or in the kitchen of a local café, hotel or restaurant.

You can choose other additional or specialist learning options to meet your personal interests and career goals. You could, for example, choose to take an option in food preparation or guest services, or take a GCSE in Food Technology or Languages. Alternatively, you could broaden your learning by studying a different subject altogether, perhaps a humanities subject or music.

During the course, you will also complete a practical project as evidence of the skills and knowledge you have developed. You could, for example, do a customer survey for a local restaurant.

As part of your generic learning, you will also continue to study English, Maths and ICT but you will study these subjects particularly for their relevance to hospitality. You also learn teamwork, self-management and presentation skills, and how to apply your knowledge and skills creatively in a business environment.

Advanced Level

The Advanced Level Diploma is normally taken in the sixth form or in a college of further education. It is equivalent to three and a half A levels and is worth 420 UCAS points.

There is also a Progression Level Diploma, which is like the Advanced Diploma, but without various options, and it is equivalent to two A levels. It is worth 300 UCAS points.

From 2011, an Extended Diploma will also be available, which will have more generic, as well as additional and specialist, learning.

After doing the Progression, Advanced or Extended Diploma you could go on to college or university, or to further training and employment.

The Diploma in Hospitality and choosing a career

A Diploma in Hospitality does not mean you have to take up a career in this sector. The Diploma is designed to give you a wide range of next-step options. After studying a Foundation or Higher Diploma in Hospitality, you might choose to do a Progression, Advanced or Extended Diploma, or perhaps do A levels. You could also do an Apprenticeship or take up a job with further training. Careers that are directly related to hospitality include bar manager/owner or publican, catering or restaurant manager, chef, fast food service assistant/manager, functions caterer, hotel manager, hotel porter, housekeeper, kitchen assistant, party organiser, and waiter/waitress.

Further information

- Hospitality Diploma website   www.hospitalitydiploma.co.uk
- British Institute of Innkeeping   www.bii.org
- Institute of Hospitality   www.instituteofhospitality.org
- Institute of Brewing and Distilling   www.ibd.org.uk
- People 1st (Sector Skills Council for Hospitality, Leisure, Travel and Tourism)   www.people1st.co.uk
- Springboard UK   www.springboarduk.org.uk
- Pilgrim, Dee, *Real Life Guide to Catering*, Trotman
- Miller, Rose, and Zajac, Camilla, *Real Life Guide to Hospitality and Events Management*, Trotman

INFORMATION TECHNOLOGY

The Diploma in IT uses a mix of theoretical and applied learning approaches to help you understand how organisations work, the role technology plays, and how to create technology solutions.

Foundation and Higher Diplomas

The Foundation Diploma is equivalent to five GCSEs at grades D–G. The Higher Diploma is equivalent to seven GCSEs at grades A*–C.

Your teachers and advisers will be able to help you decide which level is more appropriate for you at this stage of your learning.

How is the Diploma in IT taught and assessed?

The principal learning element includes:

- how technology transforms society
- how it affects the success of a business
- creating technology solutions
- designing and developing a multimedia product
- working with other people and in teams
- use of communications in business
- the roles of IT professionals and how they contribute to different industries.

You will also do a minimum of 10 days' work experience, probably in an IT-related placement, and get the chance to learn from professionals in the field.

You can choose other additional or specialist learning options to meet your personal interests and career goals. You could, for example, choose a specialist IT course in software design, web development or business administration. Alternatively, you could take a GCSE in, for example, Economics or a modern foreign language. Or, you could broaden your learning by studying a different subject altogether, perhaps a humanities subject or music.

During the course, you will also complete a practical project as evidence of the skills and knowledge you have developed. It could be a written piece of work, an investigation or something practical, such as designing and building a website for a local charity.

As part of your generic learning, you will also continue to study English, Maths and ICT but you will study these subjects particularly for their relevance to IT. You also learn teamwork, self-management and presentation skills, and how to apply your knowledge and skills creatively in a business environment.

Advanced Level

The Advanced Level Diploma is normally taken in the sixth form or in a college of further education. It is equivalent to three and a half A levels and is worth 420 UCAS points.

There is also a Progression Level Diploma, which is like the Advanced Diploma, but without various options, and it is equivalent to two A levels. It is worth 300 UCAS points.

From 2011, an Extended Diploma will also be available, which will have more generic, as well as additional and specialist, learning.

After doing the Progression, Advanced or Extended Diploma you could go on to college or university, or to further training and employment.

The Diploma in IT and choosing a career

A Diploma in IT does not mean you have to take up a career in this sector. The Diploma is designed to give you a wide range of next-step options. After studying a Foundation or Higher Diploma in IT, you might choose to do a Progression, Advanced or Extended Diploma, or perhaps do A levels. You could also do an Apprenticeship or take up a job with further training. For ideas on specific careers in IT, look at the careers pathway section on page 76.

Further information

- IT Diploma website   www.e-skills.com/Diploma-in-IT

- BBC Webwise   www.bbc.co.uk/webwise

- British Computer Society   www.bcs.org

- Computer Information Center   www.compinfo-center.com

- ICT Teacher   www.ict-teacher.com

- IT Careers   www.computeach.co.uk/Jegsworks
  www.jegsworks.com/Lessons/lessonintro.htm

- Hobbs, Mike, *E-Commerce Uncovered*, Trotman

- *How to Get Ahead In … IT and Administration*, Raintree

MANUFACTURING AND PRODUCT DESIGN

The Diploma in Manufacturing and Product Design uses a mix of theoretical and applied learning approaches to help you understand and gain knowledge about the manufacturing industry, its production systems and processes. The main areas in the sector are:

- food and drink
- textiles and clothing
- processing
- chemicals, polymers and pharmaceuticals
- engineering materials.

Foundation and Higher Diplomas

The Foundation Diploma is equivalent to five GCSEs at grades D–G. The Higher Diploma is equivalent to seven GCSEs at grades A*–C.

Your teachers and advisers will be able to help you decide which level is more appropriate for you at this stage of your learning.

How is the Diploma in Manufacturing and Product Design taught and assessed?

The principal learning element includes:

- how manufacturing businesses work and the processes they use
- the different materials and how they are used
- manufacturing in the UK and its place in global manufacturing
- product design
- business systems and enterprise.

You will also do a minimum of 10 days' work experience and get the chance to learn from professionals, probably in the manufacturing industry. You might, for example, have a work placement in a production factory or with a design team.

You can choose other additional or specialist learning options to meet your personal interests and career goals. You could, for example, choose a specialist course in manufacturing and product design, such as robot technology and how manufacturers are using it. Or, you might want to learn more business systems within the industry. Alternatively, you could broaden your learning by studying a different subject altogether, perhaps a foreign language or a humanities subject.

During the course, you will also complete a practical project as evidence of the skills and knowledge you have developed. It could be a written piece of work, an investigation or something practical, such as looking at the end product, and how it is costed, promoted and launched.

As part of your generic learning, you will also continue to study English, Maths and ICT but you will study these subjects particularly for their relevance to manufacturing and product design. You will also learn teamwork, self-management and presentation skills, and how to apply your knowledge and skills creatively in a business environment.

Advanced Level

The Advanced Level Diploma is normally taken in the sixth form or in a college of further education. It is equivalent to three and a half A levels and is worth 420 UCAS points.

There is also a Progression Level Diploma, which is like the Advanced Diploma, but without various options, and it is equivalent to two A levels. It is worth 300 UCAS points.

From 2011, an Extended Diploma will also be available, which will have more generic, as well as additional and specialist, learning.

After doing the Progression, Advanced or Extended Diploma you could go on to college or university, or to further training and employment.

The Diploma in Manufacturing and Product Design and choosing a career

A Diploma in Manufacturing and Product Design does not mean you have to take up a career in this sector. The Diploma is designed to give you a wide range of next-step options. After studying a Foundation or Higher Diploma in Manufacturing and Product Design, you might choose to do a Progression, Advanced or Extended Diploma, or perhaps do A levels. You could also do an Apprenticeship or take up a job with further training. Specific careers in manufacturing and product design include assembly work, biomedical engineering, brewing, computer-aided design draughtsman/woman, electricity generation, engineering (at different levels and in many different contexts), motor vehicle production, oil worker, and telecommunications.

Further information

- Manufacturing and Product Design Diploma website

  www.manufacturingdiploma.co.uk

- CITB-Construction Skills

  www.citb.org.uk/careers

- Cogent (Sector Skills Council for the Oil and Gas Extraction, Chemicals Manufacturing and Petroleum Industries)

  www.cogent-ssc.com/education_ and_qualifications

- e-skills UK

  www.e-skills.com/1044

- Energy Institute

  www.energyinst.org.uk

- Engineering Careers Information Service — www.enginuity.org.uk/routes_into_engineering/your_options.cfm

- Engineering Council — www.engc.org.uk

- Improve Ltd (Sector Skills Council for Food and Drink) — www.improveltd.co.uk

- Institute of Brewing and Distilling — www.ibd.org.uk

- Institute of Materials, Minerals and Mining — www.materials-careers.org.uk

- Institute of Measurement and Control — www.instmc.org.uk/young-tech-network

- Institute of Petroleum — www.petroleum.co.uk

- Institution of Agricultural Engineers — www.iagre.org

- Institution of Engineering and Technology — www.theiet.org

- Institution of Mechanical Engineers — www.imeche.org.uk

- National Centre for Training and Education in Prosthetics and Orthotics — www.strath.ac.uk/prosthetics

- Network Rail — www.networkrail.co.uk/aspx/117.aspx

- Oilcareers — www.oilcareers.com/content/training

- Royal Aeronautical Service — www.raes.org.uk

- Royal Institute of Naval Architects — www.rina.org.uk

- Scottish Engineering — www.scottishengineering.org.uk

- SEMTA (Sector Skills Council for Science, Engineering and Manufacturing Technologies) - Careers Information Service — www.semta.org.uk

PUBLIC SERVICES

The Diploma in Public Services uses a mix of theoretical and applied learning approaches to help you learn about public services, including the armed forces, education, law and order, health, and local and central government.

Foundation and Higher Diplomas

The Foundation Diploma is equivalent to five GCSEs at grades D–G. The Higher Diploma is equivalent to seven GCSEs at grades A*–C.

Your teachers and advisers will be able to help you decide which level is more appropriate for you at this stage of your learning.

How is the Diploma in Public Services taught and assessed?

The principal learning element includes:

- finding out about local and nationally delivered public services
- the job roles of people who work in public services
- how public services assess, support and promote well-being for individuals and communities
- communication in the public services
- health and well-being in the community, including safety and protection
- the skills needed to work in public services.

You will also do a minimum of 10 days' work experience, probably in a public services workplace and get the chance to learn from professionals in the sector.

You can choose other additional or specialist learning options to meet your personal interests and career goals. You could, for example, choose a topic specifically related to your public services studies, such as statistics. Alternatively, you could broaden your learning by studying a different subject altogether, perhaps a foreign language, a humanities subject, or music.

During the course, you will also complete a practical project as evidence of the skills and knowledge you have developed, for example how locally delivered public services can contribute to improving the well-being and protection of elderly people.

As part of your generic learning, you will also continue to study English, Maths and ICT but you will study these subjects particularly for their relevance to public services. You also learn teamwork, self-management and presentation skills, and how to apply your knowledge and skills creatively in a business environment.

Advanced Level

The Advanced Level Diploma is normally taken in the sixth form or in a college of further education. It is equivalent to three and a half A levels and is worth 420 UCAS points.

There is also a Progression Level Diploma, which is like the Advanced Diploma, but without various options, and it is equivalent to two A levels. It is worth 300 UCAS points.

From 2011, an Extended Diploma will also be available, which will have more generic, and additional and specialist, learning.

After doing the Progression, Advanced or Extended Diploma you could go on to college or university, or to further training and employment.

The Diploma in Public Services and choosing a career

A Diploma in Public Services does not mean you have to take up a career in this sector. The Diploma is designed to give you a wide range of next-step options. After studying a Foundation or Higher Diploma in Public Services, you might choose to do a Progression, Advanced or Extended Diploma, or perhaps do A levels. You could also do an Apprenticeship or take up a job with further training. Specific careers in public services include accountant, administrator, civil servant, clerk, finance officer, health and safety adviser, human resources officer, occupational health officer, receptionist, secretary, switchboard operator, and training officer.

Further information

- Public Services Diploma   www.diplomainpublicservices.co.uk
- Association of Medical Secretaries, Practice Managers, Administrators and Receptionists   www.amspar.co.uk
- British Safety Council   www.britishsafetycouncil.co.uk
- Civil Service Careers   www.civilservice.gov.uk/jobs
- Council for Administration Careers   www.breakintobiz
- Financial Services Authority – Careers   www.fsa.gov.uk/Pages/About/careers
- Health and Safety Executive – Careers   www.hse.gov.uk/careers
- Institute of Chartered Secretaries and Administrators   www.icsa.org.uk
- Institute of Financial Services   www.ifslearning.ac.uk
- Institute of Legal Executives   www.ilex.org.uk/about_legal_executives.aspx
- Institute of Occupational Safety and Health   www.iosh.co.uk
- Springboard UK   www.springboarduk.org.uk

RETAIL BUSINESS

The Diploma in Retail Business uses a mix of theoretical and applied learning approaches to help you learn about the retail industry and how it works, including different types of businesses and jobs, and what retail means to people and communities.

Foundation and Higher Diplomas

The Foundation Diploma is equivalent to five GCSEs at grades D–G. The Higher Diploma is equivalent to seven GCSEs at grades A*–C.

Your teachers and advisers will be able to help you decide on which level is more appropriate for you at this stage of your learning.

How is the Diploma in Retail Business taught and assessed?

The principal learning element includes:

- finding out how goods go from being manufactured to being sold in shops
- exploring how a retail outlet is run
- learning about marketing and sales targets
- sales techniques, practices and procedures
- understanding the importance of customer service
- exploring enterprise and innovation in business
- ethical and environmental issues in retail business
- the risks and problems of retail supply chains
- health and safety aspects in the sector.

You will also do a minimum of 10 days' work experience, usually in the retail business sector, and get the chance to learn from those already working in a business environment.

You can choose other additional or specialist learning options to meet your personal interests and career goals. You could, for example, choose a topic that would be helpful in retail business, such as a modern foreign language. Or, you could broaden your learning by studying a different subject altogether, perhaps music or an additional science subject.

During the course, you will also complete a practical project as evidence of the skills and knowledge you have developed, for example on the effect of particular marketing or sales techniques on customer choice.

As part of your generic learning, you will also continue to study English, Maths and ICT but you will study these subjects particularly for their relevance to retail business. You also learn teamwork, self-management and presentation skills, and how to apply your knowledge and skills creatively in a business environment.

Advanced Level

The Advanced Level Diploma is normally taken in the sixth form or in a college of further education. It is equivalent to three and a half A levels and is worth 420 UCAS points.

There is also a Progression Level Diploma, which is like the Advanced Diploma, but without various options, and it is equivalent to two A levels. It is worth 300 UCAS points.

From 2011, an Extended Diploma will also be available, which will have more generic, as well as additional and specialist, learning.

After doing the Progression, Advanced or Extended Diploma you could go on to college or university, or to further training and employment.

The Diploma in Retail Business and choosing a career

A Diploma in Retail Business does not mean you have to take up a career in this sector. The Diploma is designed to give you a wide range of next-step options. After studying a Foundation or Higher Diploma in Retail Business, you might choose to do a Progression, Advanced or Extended Diploma, or perhaps do A levels. You could also do an Apprenticeship or take up a job along with further training. Specific careers in the retail business include antiques dealer, bookseller, builder's merchant, buyer, call centre operative, car salesperson, checkout operator, customer services, market trader, sales assistant, shoe repairer, store demonstrator, store manager, trading standards officer and wine merchant.

Further information

- Retail Business Diploma website — www.diplomainretailbusiness.com/categories.php?categories_id=1

- British Shops and Stores Association Limited — www.british-shops.co.uk

- British Franchise Association — www.thebfa.org

- Chartered Institute of Marketing — www.cim.co.uk

- Chartered Institute of Purchasing and Supply — www.cips.org

- Institute of Customer Service — www.instituteofcustomerservice.com

- Institute of Direct Marketing — ww.theidm.com

- Institute of Sales Promotion — www.isp.org.uk

- Marketing and Sales Standards Setting Body — www.msssb.org

- Scottish Enterprise — www.scottish-enterprise.com

- Skillfast (Sector Skills Council for the Apparel, Footwear and Textile Industry) — www.skillfast-uk.org

- Trading Standards Institute — www.tradingstandards.gov.uk

SOCIETY, HEALTH AND DEVELOPMENT

The Diploma in Society, Health and Development offers a mix of theoretical and applied learning to help students to learn about the four sectors – health, adult social care, the children and young people's workforce, and community justice.

Foundation and Higher Diplomas

The Foundation Diploma is equivalent to five GCSEs at grades D–G. The Higher Diploma is equivalent to seven GCSEs at grades A*–C.

Your teachers and advisers will be able to help you decide which level is more appropriate for you at this stage of your learning.

How is the Diploma in Society, Health and Development taught and assessed?

The principal learning element includes:

- the values and principles involved in supporting and meeting the needs of individuals and groups of people in society
- the political, social and economic factors that affect the four sectors
- partnership working across the sector and within each sector
- communication and information-sharing
- personal and professional development in the work environment
- safeguarding and protecting individuals and society.

You will also do a minimum of 10 days' work experience in one or more of the sectors and get the chance to learn from professionals working in the area.

You can choose other additional or specialist learning options to meet your personal interests and career goals. You could, for example, choose to learn about the role of play or music, or how to handle ethical dilemmas in the management and treatment of elderly people. Alternatively, you could broaden your learning by studying a different subject altogether, perhaps a foreign language or an additional science.

During the course, you will also complete a practical project as evidence of the skills and knowledge you have developed, for example on partnership approaches to the care of people with learning difficulties.

As part of your generic learning, you will also continue to study English, Maths and ICT but you will study these subjects particularly for their relevance to society, health and development. You also learn teamwork, self-management and presentation skills.

Advanced Level

The Advanced Level Diploma is normally taken in the sixth form or in a college of further education. It is equivalent to three and a half A levels and is worth 420 UCAS points.

There is also a Progression Level Diploma, which is like the Advanced Diploma, but without various options, and it is equivalent to two A levels. It is worth 300 UCAS points.

From 2011, an Extended Diploma will also be available, which will have more generic, as well as additional and specialist, learning.

After doing the Progression, Advanced or Extended Diploma you could go on to college or university, or to further training and employment.

The Diploma in Society, Health and Development and choosing a career

A Diploma in Society, Health and Development does not mean you have to take up a career in this sector. The Diploma is designed to give you a wide range of next-step options. After studying a Foundation or Higher Diploma in Society, Health and Development, you might choose to do a Progression, Advanced or Extended Diploma, or perhaps do A levels. You could also do an Apprenticeship or take up a job with further training. There is a vast range of careers across these four sectors, including ambulance driver, audiologist, benefits adviser, care assistant, chiropodist/podiatrist, complementary health practitioner, crèche manager, critical care technologist, careers adviser, charity fundraiser, childminder, counsellor, dental hygienist (and other careers in dentistry), dietitian, education officer, healthcare assistant, health service manager, home care assistant, hospital porter, housing manager, legal executive, medical technical officer, money adviser, nurse, occupational therapist, optician, pharmacy, physiotherapist, play worker, medical practice manager, Member of Parliament, probation, officer, prosthetist/orthotist, radiographer, registrar (of births, marriages and deaths), school matron, social worker, teaching assistant, therapist, trade union official, volunteer organiser, warden (accommodation), welfare rights officer, and youth worker.

Further information

- Society, Health and Development   http://shd.skillsforhealth.org.uk
  Diploma website

- Advice UK   www.adviceuk.org.uk

- CACHE (Council for Awards in Children'   www.cache.org.uk
  Care and Education)

- Care Council for Wales   www.ccwales.org.uk

- Citizens Advice   www.adviceguide.org.uk

- Citizens Advice Scotland   www.cas.org.uk

- General Social Care Council   www.gscc.org.uk

- Institute for Complementary Medicine   www.i-c-m.org.uk

- Institute of Healthcare Management   www.ihm.org.uk

- Institute of Legal Executives   www.ilex.org.uk

- Law Society of England and Wales   www.lawsociety.org.uk

- Law Society of Northern Ireland   www.lawsoc-ni.org

- Law Society of Scotland   www.lawscot.org.uk

- NCFE   www.ncfe.org.uk

- NHS Careers   www.nhscareers.nhs.uk

- Northern Ireland Social Care Council   www.niscc.info

- Royal College of Nursing   www.learnaboutnursing.org

- Scottish Social Services Council   www.sssc.uk.com

- Skills for Health   www.skillsforhealth.org.uk

SPORT AND ACTIVE LEISURE

The Diploma in Sport and Active Leisure uses a mix of theoretical and applied learning approaches to help you to acquire knowledge, skills and understanding about the sport and active leisure industry.

Foundation and Higher Diplomas

The Foundation Diploma is equivalent to five GCSEs at grades D–G. The Higher Diploma is equivalent to seven GCSEs at grades A*–C.

Your teachers and advisers will be able to help you decide which level is more appropriate for you at this stage of your learning.

How is the Diploma in Sport and Active Leisure taught and assessed?

The principal learning element includes:

- the nature of the sport and active leisure industry and who works in it
- how the body works
- the benefits of an active and healthy lifestyle
- the importance of healthy eating and the impact of unhealthy choices
- customer service and the personal skills needed in the industry
- coaching, officiating and administration
- investigating the range of career pathways in the sport and active leisure industry.

You will also do a minimum of 10 days' work experience, usually in sport and active leisure, and get the chance to learn from professionals working in the sector.

You can choose other additional or specialist learning options to meet your personal interests and career goals. You could, for example, choose to take coaching qualifications in one or more sports. Alternatively, you could broaden your learning by studying a different subject altogether, perhaps a foreign language or music.

During the course, you will also complete a practical project as evidence of the skills and knowledge you have acquired, for example on the development of free or low-cost activities for older citizens in a sports centre.

As part of your generic learning, you will also continue to study English, Maths and ICT but you will study these subjects particularly for their relevance to sport and active leisure. You will also learn teamwork, self-management and presentation skills, and how to apply your knowledge and skills creatively in a business environment.

Advanced Level

The Advanced Level Diploma is normally taken in a sixth form or college of further education. It is equivalent to three and a half A levels and is worth 420 UCAS points.

There is also a Progression Level Diploma, which is like the Advanced Diploma, but without various options, and it is equivalent to two A levels. It is worth 300 UCAS points.

From 2011, an Extended Diploma will also be available, which will have more generic, as well as additional and specialist, learning.

After doing the Progression, Advanced or Extended Diploma you could go on to college or university, or to further training and employment.

The Diploma in Sport and Active Leisure and choosing a career

A Diploma in Sport and Active Leisure does not mean you have to take up a career in this sector. The Diploma is designed to give you a wide range of next-step options. After studying a Foundation or Higher Diploma in Sport and Active Leisure, you might choose to do a Progression, Advanced or Extended Diploma, or perhaps do A levels. You could also do an Apprenticeship or take up a job with further training. For ideas on specific careers in sport and active leisure, look at the careers pathway section on page 89.

Further information

- Sport and Active Leisure Diploma website   http://saldiploma.skillsactive.com

- BBC Science and Nature – Human Body and Mind   www.bbc.co.uk/science/humanbody

- British Association of Sport and Exercise Sciences   www.bases.org.uk

- People 1st (Sector Skills Council for Hospitality, Leisure, Travel and Tourism)   www.people1st.co.uk

- Sport England   www.sportengland.org

- UK Sport   www.uksport.gov.uk

- Dixon, Beryl, *Sport and Fitness Uncovered*, Trotman

TRAVEL AND TOURISM

The Diploma in Travel and Tourism uses a mix of theoretical and applied learning approaches to help you to develop your knowledge and understanding of the sector and to develop skills that are relevant to the industry.

Foundation and Higher Diplomas

The Foundation Diploma is equivalent to five GCSEs at grades D–G. The Higher Diploma is equivalent to seven GCSEs at grades A*–C.

Your teachers and advisers will be able to help you decide on which level is more appropriate for you at this stage of your learning.

How is the Diploma in Travel and Tourism taught and assessed?

The principal learning element includes:

- looking at modes of passenger transport and the planning of travel routes
- learning about local, national and international visitor destinations
- marketing and selling
- customer services in the sector
- working in a team
- investigating the range of career pathways in travel and tourism.

You will also do a minimum of 10 days' work experience, usually in one or two placements within the sector, and get the chance to learn from professionals in this area.

You can choose other additional or specialist learning options to meet your personal interests and career goals. You could, for example, choose a modern foreign language or a topic such as marketing. Alternatively, you could broaden your learning by studying a different subject altogether, perhaps a humanities subject or music.

During the course, you will also complete a practical project as evidence of the skills and knowledge you would have developed, for example on customising services for a particular group within the community.

As part of your generic learning, you will also continue to study English, Maths and ICT but you will study these subjects particularly for their relevance to travel and tourism. You will also learn teamwork, self-management and presentation skills, and how to apply your knowledge and skills creatively in a business environment.

Advanced Level

The Advanced Level Diploma is normally taken in the sixth form or in a college of further education. It is equivalent to three and a half A levels and is worth 420 UCAS points.

There is also a Progression Level Diploma, which is like the Advanced Diploma, but without various options, and it is equivalent to two A levels. It is worth 300 UCAS points.

From 2011, an Extended Diploma will also be available, which will have more generic, as well as additional and specialist, learning.

After doing the Progression, Advanced or Extended Diploma you could go on to college or university, or to further training and employment.

The Diploma in Travel and Tourism and choosing a career

A Diploma in Travel and Tourism does not mean you have to take up a career in this sector. The Diploma is designed to give you a wide range of next-step options. After studying a Foundation or Higher Diploma in Engineering, you might choose to do a Progression, Advanced or Extended Diploma, or perhaps do A levels. You could also do an Apprenticeship or take up a job with further training. Specific careers in travel and tourism include air cabin crew, air traffic controller, coach tour manager, courier, distribution manager, driver, entertainment manager, holiday representative, importer/exporter, merchant navy, pilot, theme park assistant/manager, tour guide, tourist information centre assistant, transport manager, and travel agency sales consultant.

Further information

- Travel and Tourism Diploma website   www.tandtdiploma.co.uk

- GoSkills (Sector Skills Council for Passenger Transport)   www.goskills.org

- People 1st (Sector Skills Council for Hospitality,   www.people1st.co.uk
  Leisure, Travel and Tourism)

CHAPTER SIX

Vocational qualifications

Vocational qualifications are qualifications that prepare you for working life, specialising in a particular occupational area or a cluster of occupations. They range from quite broad-based qualifications, where you learn skills relevant to a variety of jobs, to specialist qualifications that are designed for a particular occupational sector.

It is difficult for most schools to provide a full range of vocational courses. Many schools are now working with other partners, particularly further education colleges, to provide a range of vocational learning programmes. These programmes allow some Key Stage 4 students to follow courses that are not available at their own school. The courses lead to vocational qualifications such as GCSEs in vocational subjects or NVQs.

At Key Stage 4, such courses are usually part of a broader package of more general learning but they provide an important alternative if you feel you are ready to take another step towards preparing yourself for working life – perhaps by learning about and through work in a particular occupational area.

A wide range of vocational qualifications are accredited into the National Qualifications Framework (NQF), at the different levels. The NQF will be replaced by the Qualifications and Credit Framework (QCF) in January 2011. This will also include a wide range of vocational qualification, many of which will be those previously accredited into the NQF.

Vocational qualifications serve a variety of purposes in different sectors and at different levels, so they vary in size, level and assessment.

Which vocational qualifications can I take?

The main qualifications available in schools and colleges at Key Stage 4 are:

- BTEC Firsts
- City & Guilds Certificates
- NVQ units
- OCR Nationals
- Young Apprenticeships.

BTEC (BUSINESS TECHNOLOGY AND EDUCATION COUNCIL) QUALIFICATIONS

BTEC qualifications are run by the **Edexcel** examining body. They range from Entry level to Level 8 on the National Qualifications Framework. The most common BTEC qualification in schools is the Level 2, BTEC First.

BTEC qualifications are work-related qualifications, available in a wide range of subjects, including:

- Applied Science
- Art and Design
- Business
- Construction
- E-Business
- Engineering
- Health and Social Care
- Hospitality
- IT
- Land and Environment
- Media
- Performing Arts
- Public Services
- Retail
- Sport
- Travel and Tourism.

These qualifications provide a practical approach to learning and skills development alongside the necessary theoretical background.

You can take a BTEC qualification if you are interested in learning more about a particular sector or industry. Employers have helped design these qualifications, so that you learn the skills and knowledge that employers want. You can take the qualification either as a way of preparing for direct entry to work or as a step towards continued study at the next level – in a school, college or a more specialist vocational area.

The qualifications offer a mix of theory and practice, and often include work experience. They can take the form of (or be part of) a technical certificate, which is one of the key elements of an Apprenticeship.

How are BTEC qualifications taught and assessed?

The course normally lasts 2 years and study is unit-based. The teaching and learning styles are aimed at encouraging you to be independent and resourceful and to take responsibility for your own learning. Each course is work-based and is usually assessed by your teacher or tutor in your place of study, through assignments, case studies and practical activities. Depending on the nature and level of the particular qualification, some of your work may be assessed by external examiners. You will also produce a portfolio that shows the work you have completed. BTEC qualifications are graded Pass, Merit or Distinction.

One advantage of this unit-based course is that you will get a chance to improve your performance, if you feel that you have not done as well as you expected on first taking the unit.

You might choose to do a BTEC course if you are interested in learning more about a particular sector or industry. The qualifications offer a mix of theory and practice, and can also include some work experience

What would I expect to go on to after a BTEC First?

Since BTEC Firsts have good GCSE equivalence, there should be no problem in transferring to the A level or Diploma route when you are 16. You could also continue down the same route, on to a BTEC National, perhaps in a similar subject area. BTEC Nationals are most commonly taught in colleges of further education.

What about the implications for careers?

Taking a BTEC First in, say, Applied Science does not mean you have to take up a career in this sector. You might choose to do a BTEC National or A levels in a similar or different subject area. You could also do an Apprenticeship or take up a job with further training. For ideas on specific careers in the vocational area you are interested in, look at the relevant careers pathway sections in the directories of GCSE (Chapter Five) or Diploma (Chapter Six) courses.

CITY & GUILDS QUALIFICATIONS

City & Guilds Certificate courses are taught in some schools. They may be available at Level 1 or 2. They provide an introduction to specific areas of work, such as:

- food studies
- hair and beauty
- hospitality and catering
- IT systems support.

How is a City & Guilds Certificate taught and assessed?

Each course is work-based and will provide you with knowledge about the particular industry you are interested in. It will help you learn useful basic skills and relevant background knowledge through practical activities. The course normally lasts 1 or 2 years and study is unit-based. Units are assessed by assignments, which consist of practical tasks or activities and some testing of the background knowledge. Written tests are usually multiple choice tests. You will also collect a portfolio of evidence to demonstrate your achievements.

What would I expect to go on to from a City & Guilds course?

There should be no problem in transferring to a less specialised route, such as the Diploma, at age 16. It is also possible to progress on to a Level 2 course, such as a BTEC or OCR National in the same subject area. Such courses are most commonly taught in colleges of further education.

What do these courses mean for careers?

Taking a City & Guilds certificate in, say, Hair and Beauty does not mean you have to take up a career in this sector. You might choose to do a Diploma or a BTEC National. You could also do an Apprenticeship or take up a job with further training. For ideas on specific careers in the vocational area you are interested in, look at the relevant careers pathway sections in the directories of GCSE (Chapter Five) or Diploma (Chapter Six) courses.

NVQs (NATIONAL VOCATIONAL QUALIFICATIONS)

NVQs are work-related qualifications that are based on National Occupational Standards. They are available across a very wide range of types of work. The qualifications are designed to be delivered in the workplace or somewhere that is quite like a real working environment. NVQs are skills-based, but there is no set learning programme, which means that you can learn in a flexible way that suits your needs.

How are NVQs taught and assessed?

NVQs are not so commonly taught in schools because they are so practical in nature and need to be delivered in a realistic working environment. However, some schools are able to deliver an NVQ qualification, or units towards one, through partnership working with a college of further education, vocational learning centre or a local employer.

Assessment is evidence-based, that is, you need to prepare a portfolio to demonstrate what you have learnt and achieved. However, other methods of assessment are also used, where appropriate, for different components of the qualification.

What would I expect to go on to from an NVQ?

At Key Stage 4, any NVQ study should take up only a small part of your overall study programme. There should be no problem in progressing to a less specialised route, such as a Diploma, at age 16. But it is also possible to get on to a full NVQ programme, an Apprenticeship or a Level 2 course, such as a BTEC National in the same subject area. These programmes will normally be work-based or taught in a college of further education.

What do NVQs mean for careers?

Taking an NVQ in, say, Catering and Hospitality does not mean you have to take up a career in this sector. You might choose to go on to do a Diploma or a BTEC National. You could also decide to do an Apprenticeship or take up a job with further training. For ideas on specific careers in the vocational area you are interested in, look at the relevant careers pathway sections in the directories of GCSE (Chapter Five) or Diploma (Chapter Six) courses.

OCR NATIONALS

An OCR National (at Level 2) is a nationally recognised, work-related qualification. The National Award is equivalent to two GCSEs (A*–C), while the National Certificate is equivalent to four GCSEs (A*–C).

OCR Nationals are available in the following range of subjects:

- Art and Design
- Business
- Design
- Health and Social Care
- ICT
- Media
- Public Services
- Science
- Sport
- Travel and Tourism.

You can take an OCR National if you are interested in learning more about a particular sector or industry, but you are not quite sure about which career path to take. As with the BTECs, many have been designed in collaboration with employers. They can be taken either as a way of preparing for entry to work or as a step towards continued study at the next level.

The qualifications offer a mix of theory and practice, and often include work experience. They can take the form of (or be part of) a technical certificate, one of the key elements of an Apprenticeship.

OCR Nationals are available at Levels 1–3. At Level 2, for example, they aim to help you to perform a variety of tasks with some guidance or supervision.

How are OCR Nationals taught and assessed?

OCR Nationals take a practical approach to provide you with the skills, knowledge and understanding you need to start work, or progress to further study. OCR Nationals also help you develop your personal skills in areas that would be useful in any workplace, such as team working, communication and problem solving. The courses have been designed to give credit to your achievements and your ability to carry out tasks in a way that is relevant to your workplace.

The course normally lasts 2 years and is assessed through assignments, case studies and practical activities. There will be several different units to do, at least one of which will be compulsory. Your teachers will help you choose the units you should take.

All your work is marked by your teachers. A Moderator from the OCR Exam Board visits the school or college to check the school is assessing your work correctly and giving you the correct grade.

One advantage of such a unit-based course is that it gives you a chance to improve your performance, if you feel that you have not done as well as you expected on first taking the unit.

What would I expect to go on to from an OCR National?

Since OCR Nationals have good GCSE equivalence, there should be no problem in transferring to the A level or Diploma route when you are 16. You could also go on to a BTEC National or a higher-level OCR National, perhaps in a similar subject area. BTEC Nationals and the higher-level OCR Nationals are most commonly taught in colleges of further education.

What do OCR Nationals mean for careers?

Taking an OCR National in, say, Business does not mean you have to take up a career in this sector. You might choose to do a higher-level OCR National, a BTEC National or A levels in a similar or different subject area. You could also do an Apprenticeship or take up a job with further training. For ideas on specific careers in the vocational area you are interested in, look at the relevant careers pathway sections in the directories of GCSE (Chapter Five) or Diploma (Chapter Six) courses.

YOUNG APPRENTICESHIPS

Young Apprenticeships are vocational programmes available across a range of subject areas in some schools and colleges. Schools and colleges act in partnership to offer Young Apprenticeship programmes, so you would need to find out whether your school is part of a Young Apprenticeship partnership. In these courses, which are meant for 14–16 year olds, you will follow an applied learning programme that is specific to your chosen learning area. These courses form a significant part of the Key Stage 4 study programme (typically, you would spend 2 days each week on the course), but you will also have to complete a programme of core studies within the National Curriculum, including English, Mathematics, ICT and Science. Young Apprenticeship programmes last for the full 2-year period of Key Stage 4.

Young Apprenticeships are available in the following learning areas:

- Art and Design
- Business and Administration
- Construction
- Engineering
- Hairdressing
- Health and Social Care
- Motor Industry
- Performing Arts.

How are Young Apprenticeships taught and assessed?

The course takes up 2 days a week (or equivalent) over the 2 years of the programme, which includes 50 days' work experience. You would do a large part of the work outside school. You will learn the theoretical aspects of the subject in your school, a college or with a training provider, but you will also work a total of 50 days in a workplace with an employer, learning work skills. The 50 days may be in week-blocks or 1 day a week depending on local partnership arrangements.

Overall, learning is through a mixture of classroom lessons, practical training and work experience. The course includes taking Level 2 qualifications in the specific vocational area: you might take a GCSE in a vocational subject (worth two GCSEs) or another type of vocational qualification, such as an NVQ or a technical certificate. You may do a combination of qualifications, depending on how the local partnership programme is designed. As part of the work experience, you may be required to complete a Level 2 work-based project. Each programme also provides additional enterprise and enrichment opportunities.

What would I expect to go on to from a Young Apprenticeship?

If you do a Young Apprenticeship, usually you move directly into employment. Most often this will be via a full Apprenticeship. The qualifications you will have gained may help you to move on to an accelerated post-16 Apprenticeship in your chosen area.

However, you could also decide to stay on in full-time education, either at school or college. Taking a Young Apprenticeship programme does not mean you have to take the Apprenticeship route. It's always possible to change your thinking about careers and move on in a different direction – either to a different vocational pathway or back onto a more general educational programme that will keep your options for longer. But remember that if you are well into the programme when you do decide you want a change, it may be difficult to restructure your study programme at that stage.

What does a Young Apprenticeship mean for careers?

Taking a Young Apprenticeship in, say, Engineering does not mean you have to take up a career in this sector. You might choose to do a Diploma or A levels. As suggested above, most Young Apprenticeship learners will go on to do a full Apprenticeship or take up a job with further training. For ideas on specific careers in the vocational area you are interested in, look at the relevant careers pathway sections in the directories of GCSE (Chapter Five) or Diploma (Chapter Six) courses.

OTHER VOCATIONAL QUALIFICATIONS

There are many other vocational courses that schools or colleges offer outside the above categories. Some of them take the form of 'taster' courses, providing a basic introduction to an occupational sector. These do not usually lead to a formal qualification.

CHAPTER SEVEN

Entry qualifications

What subjects are available as Entry qualifications?

Entry level is the first tier on the National Qualifications and Credit Framework. Entry level qualifications are nationally recognised qualifications. They measure achievement below GCSE grade G and Level 1 on the National Qualifications Framework. There are no entry requirements and they may be suitable for you if you are not yet ready to take qualifications in one or more area of learning at Level 1. Taking these qualifications should help you build basic knowledge and skills to apply your learning in everyday situations.

You can take Entry level qualifications at three sub-levels: Entry 1, Entry 2 and Entry 3. These levels are broadly the same as the National Curriculum Levels 1, 2 and 3.

More than 100 Entry level certificates or awards are available, in a wide range of subjects, though there will probably only be a limited choice in your local school, college or partnership.

Entry level qualifications available nationally can be grouped in four broad areas:

- English, Science and Mathematics
- literacy, numeracy and life skills
- general vocational subjects that offer a broad introduction to the world of work
- vocational subjects that introduce you to a particular area of work, such as retail, hairdressing or office practice.

One example of such an Entry qualification is the CACHE Entry Level Certificate in Preparation for Childcare, which is sometimes offered by schools or school–college partnerships.

You can study Entry level qualifications at a pace that suits you; there is no set period for completing them. Entry level certificates in National Curriculum subjects such as English, Mathematics and Science usually take 1 or 2 years to complete in Years 10 or 11.

You can study for Entry level qualifications in a school or a further education college, but they can also be taken in other community settings, such as a local learning centre.

How are Entry level qualifications taught and assessed?

Entry level certificates or awards are graded Entry 1, Entry 2 or Entry 3. Each course consists of a series of topics or units, taught in a practical, hands-on way. Each unit is assessed separately, which means that your achievements are recognised as you progress through the units. You are assessed by a combination of tests, assignments and tasks – written, oral and practical. You can choose to re-take individual units at any time.

You may also have to make a portfolio that shows evidence of what you have achieved. It will contain things such as witness statements (a written or oral account of your performance by another person), video, audio and photographs. The portfolio is assessed by your teacher. Different subjects and courses vary in structure, content and the number of units. When you complete all the units, you get the full certificate or award.

What would I expect to go on to from Entry level qualifications?

Entry level qualifications are not focused towards particular jobs, but they do support your progress towards life after school. You can progress from one Entry level to the next. Then, at Entry 3, the qualifications are designed to help you move on to related qualifications at Level 1 of the National Qualifications Framework, such as:

- GCSEs
- Key Skills
- Skills for Life
- NVQs
- BTEC Introductory or Level 1 BTEC Awards, Certificates or Diplomas.

They can also lead to work-based learning (such as an Apprenticeship) or straight into a job.

What do Entry level qualifications mean for careers?

Taking an Entry qualification does not limit your choice of employment, even if you are taking an Entry qualification in a vocational area. The qualification is a pre-vocational or preliminary qualification and you will have plenty of time to re-think about which sector of work might be most suitable for you.

Remember, at Entry 3, the qualifications help you move on to related qualifications at Level 1 of the National Qualifications Framework, such as:

- BTEC Introductory or Level 1 Awards, Certificates or Diplomas
- GCSEs
- Key Skills
- NVQs
- Skills for Life.

Entry level qualifications can also lead to work-based learning, for example, an Apprenticeship or straight into a job.

If you do already have some ideas about the sort of direction you would like to take in the world of work, you can look at the relevant careers pathway section in the pages covering GCSEs or the Diplomas (which do include jobs for people leaving school with Entry qualifications).

PART THREE

END NOTE

CHAPTER EIGHT

What next?

This chapter will give you some more information about the options open to you after your Key Stage 4 qualifications.

At the present time, compulsory schooling ends in the UK at age 16. However, the government is in the process of changing this. It favours the idea of all young people staying in some form of learning post-16. It has passed new laws which mean that:

- young people in Year 8 in 2009/10 will continue in education or training until they are 17 years old
- those in Year 7 (who started secondary school in September 2009) will continue to stay in learning until they are 18 years old.

This change does not necessarily mean you have to stay in school. You will be able to choose between:

- full-time education, such as in school or in college
- work-based learning, such as an apprenticeship
- part-time education or training, if you have been employed or self-employed or have been volunteering for more than 20 hours a week.

In any case, once you've chosen your Key Stage 4 qualifications, it won't be long before you have to think about what to do afterwards. You may even have some thoughts about this already, especially if you have a particular career pathway in mind. Here are some of the options.

GCE A levels and AS levels

GCE A levels remain the most widely followed post-16 qualification. They are seen as the traditional gateway to higher education for most students, although there are other excellent routes (Diplomas, BTEC Nationals, International Baccalaureate, etc). A levels offer considerable flexibility of choice, with AS and A2 programmes. You can decide:

- which subjects you would like to study
- whether you want to complete a full A level or to study a subject for 1 year (and taking an AS level) before deciding whether to study the second year and completing the A level.

A levels consist of two parts: the AS and the A2. The Advanced Subsidiary (AS) is a stand-alone qualification: it can be taken on its own and without progression onto the A2 stage (the second half of a full A level qualification). AS level consists of three units (assessed at the standard expected for a student halfway through an A level course). These units contribute 50% of the full A level qualification. Most units are assessed by examination, but some are assessed through coursework or controlled assessment. The percentage of coursework varies between different A levels, but is unlikely to exceed 20–30%.

The AS tends to cover the less demanding material in an A level course, while the A2 covers the more demanding material. For example, in the A2 you might:

- specialise in an area you studied at AS
- extend your knowledge and understanding of the subject by studying new topics
- improve your skills further.

Also, in the A2 you would combine knowledge, understanding and skills from across the A level course.

Applied A levels

'Applied' versions of the A level course are available in a few subjects:

- Art and Design
- Business Studies
- Engineering
- Health and Social Care
- ICT
- Leisure Studies
- Media
- Performing Arts
- Science
- Travel and Tourism.

Applied A levels are designed to develop your knowledge, skills and understanding in a broad vocational area. Learning is expected to be active, usually with some input from employers. Applied A levels are therefore an excellent preparation for further study or training.

Both A levels and Applied A levels are acceptable for entry into higher education. However, if you are planning to enter higher education on a particular course it is always important to check the entry requirements.

AEA (Advanced Extension Award) in Maths

AEAs were designed to challenge the top 10% of A level students, ensuring that they were tested against standards that equal the most demanding standards in other countries. They used to be available in 19 different subjects, but changes to A levels (aimed at better differentiation) led to the decision to drop AEAs, except in Mathematics.

So if you are expecting to get an A grade in A level Mathematics, you could think about taking an Advanced Extension Award (AEA) which requires a greater depth of understanding than A level.

Advanced Diplomas

We talked about Diplomas in an earlier section of this book. Advanced Level Diplomas are normally only available in the sixth form or a college of further education. Each Advanced Diploma is equivalent to three and a half A levels and is worth 420 UCAS points.

The timetable for the introduction of the Advanced Diplomas is similar to that for the Foundation and Higher Diplomas that are available at Key Stage 4. For further details, see page 99.

There is also a Progression Level Diploma, which is like the Advanced Diploma, but without various options, and it is equivalent to two A levels. It is worth 300 UCAS points.

From 2011, an Extended Diploma will also be available, which will have more generic, as well as additional and specialist, learning.

After doing a Progression, Advanced or Extended Diploma you could go on to college or university, or to further training and employment.

International Baccalaureate (IB)

The International Baccalaureate Organisation offers a 2-year programme of international education for students aged 16–19. The qualification is an excellent preparation for higher education study and is widely recognised by the world's leading universities.

Following the 2-year curriculum of the IB Diploma programme, students are encouraged to:

- ask challenging questions
- learn how to learn
- develop a strong sense of their own identity and culture
- develop the ability to communicate with and understand people from other countries and cultures.

Re-taking GCSEs

It is possible to re-take GCSEs. This may be a good idea, but only if you have solid reasons for thinking you can do better second time round. For example, you might feel that your progress through Key Stage 4 was hampered through illness or by your reaction to family trauma of some sort. Or, you might feel that you really did not do enough work and will be better motivated if you do go for re-takes. In this case especially, you might want to consider taking a mix of subjects where you need better grades and one or more new subjects that might serve to give you a new motivation.

Low grades at GCSE could also mean that GCSEs are not the right qualification for you and that you would do better to consider an alternative learning programme, for example a BTEC or an Apprenticeship.

The awarding bodies do offer some English, Mathematics and Science syllabuses for examination in November. If you are ready to move on but need to improve your grade in one of these core subjects, you can think about doing a re-sit in November. Further details of the availability of November re-sits can be obtained from the awarding bodies.

Finally, if you are thinking about re-taking GCSEs, remember that you can carry forward your moderated controlled assessment marks for one re-take. This is within a 12-month period following the initial issue of results.

BTEC qualifications

See also the entry under BTEC qualifications on page 134.

Post-16, BTEC offers a BTEC First (1-year course) and a BTEC National (2-year course).

The BTEC First is a Level 2 qualification which can be used to help you get into training or employment, or to move into the next stage of study (which might be a BTEC National, Applied A level, or other option).

BTEC Nationals are vocational qualifications to prepare students equally for direct entry into employment or for progression to higher education. The qualification comes in three forms, all at NQF Level 3: BTEC National Award, BTEC National Certificate and BTEC National Diploma.

The BTEC Diploma can also be used to get into training or employment. As it's equivalent to A levels, you can go on to higher education options.

OCR Nationals

OCR Nationals are available post-16, usually in further education colleges. See entry for OCR Nationals on page 138.

Further education

You might tend to think first about staying on at your school beyond 16 – if it has a sixth form. If you feel you want to move out the school environment, going to a further education college would be a new and interesting challenge. Some further education colleges offer A level options with a range of vocational alternatives (including BTECs and NVQs), and most also offer vocational qualifications in areas such as catering, engineering, hair and beauty, or leisure and tourism.

If you want to follow a particular career such as agriculture or horticulture you may want to attend a specialised college. These colleges run courses only in a particular vocational area. Attending a specialised college could mean you have to travel a lot or live in or near the college during the week in term time.

To help you decide which institution to study at, further education colleges (like schools with sixth forms) produce a prospectus that tells you what subjects and qualifications they can offer. They also hold open days, where you can find out more about the institution, talk to subject tutors and ask any questions you may have.

Your local school–college partnership may also have an online prospectus that lists all the 16+ options in your area. You can find your local 14–19 prospectus by visiting http://yp.direct.gov.uk/14–19prospectus.

Apprenticeships

Apprenticeships give young people the opportunity to leave full-time education and take up on-the-job training. Doing an Apprenticeship means that you learn on the job: you study for a nationally recognised qualification and earn money while you learn. There are different types of Apprenticeship available, but they all lead to one or more of the following qualifications:

- National Vocational Qualifications (NVQs)
- Key Skills qualifications
- a technical qualification such as a BTEC or City & Guilds.

There are over 180 Apprenticeships available across more than 80 industrial sectors. They cover areas such as:

- administration
- agriculture
- construction
- customer service, retailing and wholesaling
- engineering
- finance, insurance and real estate
- health and beauty
- manufacturing
- media and printing
- recreation and travel
- transportation.

National Vocational Qualifications (NVQs)

In NVQs you learn mainly through practical, work-related tasks that are designed to help you develop the skills and knowledge to do a job effectively. NVQs normally feature plenty of work-based learning and most often include some study at work or college. You can also take an NVQ qualification at Level 2 or 3 as part of an Apprenticeship.

There are over 1,300 different NVQs. They are available in many business sectors, including:

- business and management
- construction and property
- engineering
- food, catering and leisure services
- health and social care
- manufacturing, production and engineering
- sales, marketing and distribution
- sport and recreation.

They are linked to specific jobs, e.g. hairdresser or plumber.

NVQs are based on national standards for various occupations. The standards say what a competent person in a job could be expected to do. As you progress through the course, you compare your skills and knowledge with these standards. This way, you can see what you need to do to meet the standards.

You take NVQs at a pace that suits your needs, so there is no maximum time limit for the completion of an NVQ. But usually you take about 1 year to complete an NVQ at Level 1 and 2, and around 2 years for an NVQ at Level 3.

Completing an NVQ can lead to further training at the next NVQ level. You could go all the way to a Level 5 NVQ and/or professional qualifications, usually in a related area. If you've studied an NVQ at Level 3, you could also go on to a higher education course in a related vocational area.

How are NVQs taught and assessed?

NVQs are available at Levels 1–5 on the National Qualifications Framework. They are assessed on practical assignments and a portfolio of evidence. Normally, a qualified assessor will observe you and question you about the real work you did in the workplace (or a realistic working environment). They will test your knowledge and understanding as well as your actual performance. Your assessor will sign off individual units within the NVQ when you have reached the required standard. The assessment will tell you whether you are 'competent' or 'not yet competent'.

Other vocational qualifications

There are many other vocational courses and qualifications, in areas such as art and design (e.g. Diploma in Foundation Studies) and working with children (e.g. CACHE Diploma). You can find out more about these and others via the websites listed below.

Straight into employment

If you are reaching age 16 and leaving school before 2013, it will still be possible to go straight into paid employment at 16+. However, it is generally best that you do not take this option unless your employer is offering some kind of accredited further training or learning. This might be an Apprenticeship, leading to an NVQ or a BTEC qualification. We are always hearing about a few entrepreneurs who have managed to carve out a very successful career without the benefit of formal qualifications, but this is probably getting harder – and there are usually more and better options available to you if you do have some qualifications as evidence of your knowledge, skills and understanding.

How to find out more

* Apprenticeships — www.apprenticeships.org.uk
* BTEC — www.edexcel.org.uk
* CACHE Diploma — www.cache.org.uk
* Careers Wales — www.careerswales.com
* Connexions — www.connexions-direct.com
* **DCSF** Qualifications for schools and colleges — www.direct.gov.uk/en/Education And Learning/QualificationsExplained/index.htm?sId=1
* Diploma in Foundation Studies — www.edexcel.com/quals/Pages/qual-home.aspx
* Edexcel — wwwedexcel.org.uk
* Education Maintenance Allowance — http://ema.direct.gov.uk
* International Baccalaureate — www.ibo.org
* Learndirect — http://careersadvice-findacourse1.direct.gov.uk
* NVQs — www.qcda.gov.uk/6640.aspx
* Student AS/A level guide (QCDA) — www.qcda.gov.uk/4127.aspx
* UK250 (links to FE college websites) — www.uk250.co.uk/College

CHAPTER NINE

Useful contacts and sources of further information

Each country in the UK has a regulatory body for exam qualifications. These regulators are responsible for the qualification criteria and subject criteria for each examined course (including GCSEs) and they oversee what the exam boards do. Part of their job is to monitor and ensure standards.

England

In England, the regulator is Ofqual (the Office of the Qualifications and Examinations Regulator):

Ofqual
Spring Place
Coventry Business Park
Herald Avenue
Coventry CV5 6UB
Helpline: 0300 303 3346
Email: info@ofqual.gov.uk
Website: www.ofqual.gov.uk

Wales

Wales has the Department for Education, Lifelong Learning and Skills (DCELLS). Its regulatory section can be contacted at:

Department for Children, Education, Lifelong Learning and Skills (DCELLS)
Qualifications Curriculum Learning Improvement (QCLI) DivisionTy'r Afon
Various locations across Wales (see http://wales.gov.uk/contact_us/bydept/childedlifelearn/?lang=en)
English tel: 0300 0603300 or 0845 010 3300.
Welsh tel: 0300 0604400 or 0845 010 4400
Website: http://new.wales.gov.uk

Northern Ireland

In Northern Ireland the regulatory authority is the Council for the Curriculum, Examinations and Assessments (**CCEA**):

CCEA
29 Clarendon Road
Clarendon Dock
Belfast BT1 3BG
Tel: 028 9026 1200
Website: www.ccea.org.uk

Information about criteria for exam specifications is available from each of the websites.

Exam boards

AQA
Stag Hill House
Guildford GU2 7XJ
Tel: 01483 300152
Email: mailbox@aqa.org.uk
Website: www.aqa.org.uk

ASDAN
Wainbrook House
Hudds Vale Road
Bristol BS5 7HY
Tel: 0117 941 1126
Email: info@asdan.org.uk
Website: www.asdan.org.uk

Edexcel
One90 High Holborn
London WC1V 7BH
Tel: 0870 240 9800
Email: info@edexcel.org.uk
Website: www.edexcel.org.uk

OCR
1 Hills Road
Cambridge CB1 2EU
Tel: 01223 553998
Email: general.qualifications@ocr.org.uk
Website: www.ocr.org.uk

WJEC
245 Western Avenue
Cardiff CF5 2YX
Tel: 029 2026 5000
Email: info@wjec.co.uk
Website: www.wjec.co.uk